I have a growing suspicion that the antireligious sentiment, which is so pervasive in Western culture and is captured by the mantra, "I'm not religious, but I'm spiritual," is simply the latest version of that old enemy and heresy, Gnosticism. It's like saying, "I love football; I'm just not into the organized kind." Unless our faith is rooted in and structured around practices and pathways that have stood the test of time—unless it is, in some real and deep sense, *religious*—it will not hold together. Indeed, the root of the word *religion* is exactly that: to *re-ligament*, to tie broken things back together. Greg Paul's book *Resurrecting Religion* comes just in the nick of time. Greg—who claims to be neither theologian nor writer, but who does both these things brilliantly—speaks winsomely, urgently, convincingly about our need to reclaim our religious identity and heritage, while also doing what Jesus and the prophets did: rejecting all bad religion. This is a book for our times if ever there were one.

MARK BUCHANAN
Author of *Your Church Is Too Safe*

In this book, Greg Paul speaks an urgently contemporary word about the church. He knows about the church. He knows its faults: excessive accommodation to culture, privatism that is mostly irrelevant, and intellectual schemes remote from reality. But he also knows better than that. His pages teem with testimony about "the other shoe" of gospel obedience that lives in the real world, that moves in ways of mercy, compassion, and justice, and that heals and transforms. Paul is a story teller; he has rich, concrete, compelling tales about real people living out gospel lives. His book is a treasure house of evidence that there is a way that need not yield to "bad religion." We will not want to miss out on this rich testimony!

WALTER BRUEGGEMANN
Columbia Theological Seminary

It's easy to criticize religion. It's an entirely different thing to offer thought-provoking insights of your own religious practice from the trenches. Deep inside the muck and mire of human existence is where the gospel first gave light and the religious impulse was born anew—one that would care for widows and orphans in their distress and spark a living faith in a living God. Greg Paul lights up the dark realities of our post-religious talk with the hope of a religion that matters in real life to real people, right now.

DANIELLE STRICKLAND
Author of *The Ultimate Exodus*

Greg Paul's central premise, that *true religion* is vital for the life and salvation of the world, is backed by an experiential authority that is uncomfortably hard to dismiss. Particularly, reading the book of James through the lens of the Beatitudes is a lesson I'll not soon forget. This is a timely and important book.

STEVE BELL
Singer, songwriter

"True religion," writes Greg Paul, "is to faith what voice is to a thought. It puts flesh on the bones of faith." This book describes the gritty intersection between incarnational theology and integrated spirituality. With raw vulnerability and buckets full of hope, Greg Paul will restore your faith in the church.

STEVE WIENS
Senior pastor of Genesis Covenant Church, author
of *Beginnings* and *Whole*

I highly recommend that you read *Resurrecting Religion* for these reasons: stories that will move and inspire you; insight that is wise and practical; writing that is vivid and lucid; a guide (Greg) whom you'll enjoy spending time with and who has lived this story with integrity and by grace; and, finally, because this book will give you a vision for more faithfully loving your neighbors in response to our common prayer that God's Kingdom will come on earth as in heaven.

KENT ANNAN
Author of *Slow Kingdom Coming*

Resurrecting Religion will inspire you to live out the biblical call to justice and Jesus' teachings from the Sermon on the Mount. In a world that continues to create distance between the rich and poor, Greg's book teaches us the importance and power of having close relationships with those living on the margins of society.

AARON GRAHAM
Lead pastor, The District Church

resurrecting

religion

Finding Our Way Back
to the Good News

greg paul

NAVPRESS.

A NavPress resource published in alliance
with Tyndale House Publishers, Inc.

NAVPRESS○

NavPress is the publishing ministry of The Navigators, an international Christian organization and leader in personal spiritual development. NavPress is committed to helping people grow spiritually and enjoy lives of meaning and hope through personal and group resources that are biblically rooted, culturally relevant, and highly practical.

For more information, visit www.NavPress.com.

Resurrecting Religion: Finding Our Way Back to the Good News

Copyright © 2018 by Greg Paul. All rights reserved.

A NavPress resource published in alliance with Tyndale House Publishers, Inc.

NAVPRESS and the NAVPRESS logo are registered trademarks of NavPress, The Navigators, Colorado Springs, CO. *TYNDALE* is a registered trademark of Tyndale House Publishers, Inc. Absence of ® in connection with marks of NavPress or other parties does not indicate an absence of registration of those marks.

The Team:
Don Pape, Publisher
David Zimmerman, Acquisitions Editor
Helen Macdonald, Copyeditor

Cover photograph of hands copyright © by Nico Beard/Bossfight.co. All rights reserved.

Cover photograph of cross copyright © Merydolla/Shutterstock. All rights reserved.

Published in association with the literary agency of Daniel Literary Group, LLC, Nashville, TN 37215.

Some of the anecdotal illustrations in this book are true to life and are included with the permission of the persons involved. All other illustrations are composites of real situations, and any resemblance to people living or dead is purely coincidental.

For information about special discounts for bulk purchases, please contact Tyndale House Publishers at csresponse@tyndale.com, or call 1-800-323-9400.

Cataloging-in-Publication Data is available.

ISBN 978-1-63146-666-3

Printed in the United States of America

24	23	22	21	20	19	18
7	6	5	4	3	2	1

For the Beatitudes people of Sanctuary Toronto,
who for twenty-five years have been teaching me
what the church is supposed to look like.

✝

contents

introduction

SOME TIME AGO I attended a conference hosted by an organization whose primary focus is church planting. Most of the three hundred or so attendees were church planters, domestic missionaries, pastors, or people otherwise engaged in full-time mission work.

I had been invited as one of three plenary speakers. I was slated to speak to the whole gathering and to lead two seminar sessions. Writing books and speaking are not my primary gigs—what I write and talk about grows out of my day-to-day commitment to be present and participate in the Sanctuary community, as both member and pastor. Because our community holds, at its center, people who are poor, homeless, street involved, addicted, mentally ill, and in one way or another rejected by society, it is a demanding yet strangely fulfilling place to be. And consequently, I don't tend to hang around much when I have a speaking engagement. I do what I've been invited to do, then go home, where my real life is unfolding.

On this occasion, though, I came early for the express

purpose of listening to one of the other plenary speakers, whom I had never heard before. He's well known as a terrific communicator and Bible teacher. The teaching pastor of a large church, he was addressing this particular group for the first time, and he'd been asked (I think) to outline a basic theology of the gospel.

The morning started, as such events usually do, with a welcome, announcements, and then some music. Later, there would be a band, but perhaps in deference to the earliness of the hour, one talented young guy with a guitar led us through thoughtfully chosen worship songs. Scripture was read, the needs of some individuals and some challenging international situations were mentioned, and we prayed together about them.

Then the speaker got up to do his thing. He came as advertised: intelligent, articulate, witty, engaging—all of that. He spoke, it was obvious, from a deep and thoughtful conviction. The audience enjoyed him immensely.

The centerpiece of his theology of the gospel was this: *Jesus came to abolish religion.* If I'm not mistaken, he'd written a book about it. Jesus good; religion bad.

I looked around. Many heads were bobbing in assent, and there was much smiling and some occasional laughter. The speaker's audience was right there with him. I thought about who the audience members were—good people who had committed their lives to living out the gospel—and I thought about why they were there. They certainly weren't in it for the money! I reflected on what we had been doing through the course of the morning so far: catching up with one another over coffee and muffins in the foyer; gathering in a church auditorium; communally worshiping, reading Scripture, and praying; and listening to a gifted person exposit the gospel.

And I wondered, *What is it we think we're doing here? Isn't all this, um, religion? Wouldn't anybody else say this is religious activity? Simply saying that we're not religious doesn't make it so. Are we fooling ourselves?*

And I found myself asking, *What do we mean by "religion," then? And what about it scares us so much?*

It seems to me that what critics of religion—believers and nonbelievers alike—generally mean by *religion* is "all the bad, crazy, or self-important things people do in the name of God." Hypocrisy, materialism, exclusivity, judgmental attitudes, seeking or abusing power—along with the blind and dangerous arrogance that comes from believing that "God is on our side." Those attitudes and actions *are* wrongheaded and even hateful.

But is that all religion means? Didn't Jesus say that he came not to abolish the law but to fulfill it?[1] Wouldn't we have to admit that the law of Moses was religious? Didn't Jesus tell his disciples, "If you love me, you will keep my commandments"?[2] Sure, that's relationship, but isn't it also religion— actually doing what our Master asks?

Much Christian activity really is contrary to what Jesus taught. Just picking at random, let's say, supporting wars and building big, expensive edifices that serve nobody but once-a-week attendees, while children in the same city go hungry. Based on the general divergence between what our Master taught and what we often do, I would imagine that adherents of other religions routinely ignore the tenets of their faiths too.

But not all religious activity is contrary to what Jesus taught. "Religion" *does*, for instance, feed the poor. At Sanctuary—the faith community in Toronto that is my home—about twenty-five thousand meals each year are shared by a handful of people who are wealthy (relatively speaking) and a large group who are poor. Churches, missions, synagogues, mosques, and temples across our city do the same, and I know that such material care is similarly offered by faith-based groups all around the world to people who are poor. In fact, the biggest provider of support to people living in poverty, after government, is the church. Isn't that religion too?

When Christians rush to the scene of the latest world disaster with money, food, medical help, and other resources—people acting out publicly and communally what they believe privately and individually—isn't that religion?

If we deny religion, are we denying the good stuff as well as the bad? Are we, perhaps, giving ourselves permission to believe but not do much about what we believe?

Despite all its (deserved) bad press, when the church acts like the body of Christ (as it's supposed to), it does some really good stuff. My own thoughts about the matter have not been shaped in a vacuum—or at theological or church-planting conferences, which can sometimes be dangerously close to the same thing. Lived experience among the people of Sanctuary, and the long years of reflection that have accompanied that experience, has continually challenged and refined my paradigm, forcing me over and over to abandon my assumptions and forge new ways of thinking and doing. Throughout this book, stories from that crazy, dysfunctional gospel community will provide jumping-off points for ideas or illustrations of what it might look like when we actually try to live out together the things we say we believe. Each story may not always make sense right away, but just try to roll with it.

Dictionary definitions of *religion* tend to identify three characteristics: (1) belief in a god or gods (2) an organized system of beliefs (doctrines) about that god or those gods and (3) the activities, individual and communal, motivated by those beliefs.

Belief in God? Check. That's us. System of beliefs? Well, we argue enough about them and like to write them up in statements of faith that members must sign, so yes, I guess that's us too. Activities? Worship, prayer, Bible study, small groups, Sunday school, mission trips . . . uh-huh.

I'm afraid the verdict is in: Like it or not, we're religious. What are we going to do about it?

bad religion

THE SPICY TANG of weed drifts on the night air as I approach the house. I give a mental shrug—probably for the best; it should calm him down some. He's sitting on a plastic chair in the shadows on the narrow porch, as far away from the stairs and entrance to the house as possible. Mike looks up from beneath the brim of his fedora, and I catch a glimpse of his face set hard and furious before it crumbles at the sight of me.

I've known Mike for twenty years, since the days when he lived in a lean-to hidden in the wooded area beside Rosedale Valley Road. We've become close friends through the years, and nobody on God's green earth has ever taught me more about what it really looks like to live by faith. It's one thing to claim it when you've been given the comfort of security and every advantage and opportunity, as I had; it's of a different order entirely when you've grown up with abuse, addictions, home-lessness, time spent in jail, and the steady rain of indignities that saturate a life on the streets.

He begins talking before I'm all the way up the steps, the words spewing out of him, his voice rising to a kind of high-pitched quiet shriek—equal parts lament, accusation, and threat. Grief and anger throttle his vocal chords. He zigzags like a water bug over the surface of his beefs: Danny's being a jerk; he needs his dog; those crackers are the real criminals—they would never have called the cops themselves; he can't live like this and needs to go home; he was only trying to clean things up a bit; he's not leaving—has nowhere to go. And then the end of the tirade: He's dying—doesn't anybody get this? If Danny wants to play the hard man . . . Mike can't believe it himself yet.

Slow down, I tell him. Breathe. We'll figure it out. What happened? Some kind of household tiff that got out of hand. Hardly surprising, given the circumstances—Mike and Danny were old-school tough guys back in the day, among the hard-est of the hard boys out on the streets and in the jails. Where they come from, you can never afford to back down, and all the edges and instincts they've built are still there. It'll get really ugly if it gets physical. Eventually, I leave Mike lighting a cigarette and go inside to talk to Danny.

Danny is calm and quiet—and unequivocal: Mike's going to have to go. In the morning, if he can just come in and go straight to bed. Feels bad because the guy is going through some really nasty stuff, the worst, and no wonder he's snap-ping, but if he stays, it'll be a total gong show. Danny is wearing only track pants despite the coolness of the night, and I wonder to myself if this is an alpha-dog kind of thing, although his demeanor is surprisingly gentle. I understand his position, though; I do. I'd say the same thing. Bear is staying in his room and staying out of this mess. That's something.

Megna, the other Mike, appears out of the kitchen. He's clearly a little freaked out—doesn't have the same street background as the others and isn't used to this kind of volatility. He tells me Cook is on his way—Megna called him before he knew Danny had phoned me, but I'm grateful. A little dispassionate and highly competent backup will certainly be welcome if this thing goes sideways. And it still could.

I head back out to the porch. Mike, sitting there beneath his fedora, his jaw and the bones of his eye sockets a line drawing in shadow. The streetlight silvering the smoke of his cigarette, and the tears tracking down the hollows of his cheeks.

I'M NOT THEM

Maybe it happens to you, too: You're having a conversation with somebody you don't know all that well, and somehow the topic comes around to God stuff. It might be that you mention going to church or quote from the Bible. If you're one of those rare individuals who is comfortable doing so, you might actually be "witnessing," but most of us are being cautious, uncertain of what the other person's perspective is. You don't want to offend or, frankly, make an idiot of yourself.

At some point the individual cocks his or her head and, after a momentary pause, asks, "So, you're religious?"

If that person had said, "Sounds like you're spiritual,"

or asked, "Are you a follower of Jesus?" it would have been simple to answer with, "Well, yeah."

It's that word, *religious*. It conjures up images of the Crusades and whacked-out TV preachers selling prayer hankies and fringe lunatics burning copies of the Quran while proclaiming God's hate-of-the-week. It doesn't at all express the way you approach your own faith.

So we chuckle nervously, people like you and me, and mutter about being a Christian, yes, a seeker—it's more of a faith *journey*—and wind it up with "I wouldn't say I'm religious, really, but I have a personal relationship with Jesus Christ, which is a different sort of thing . . ."

While people such as Bill Maher and Christopher Hitchens (or my latest fave, the Amazing Atheist on YouTube) may offend us with their rudest statements about God and Christianity, we find ourselves also recognizing some painful truth in what they have to say. Sure, they make taking cheap shots at the looniest aspects of the church their stock-in-trade; there are, sadly, a distressing number of easy targets in organized religion. But that's the point—*we don't want to be lumped in with those wing nuts!* They are not us!

Of course, a clever guy such as Maher would say, "Really? You mentioned a 'personal relationship with Jesus Christ.' You mean the Jesus Christ who died a couple of thousand years ago? Do you converse regularly with his ghost, or is he more of an imaginary friend?"

And we would sigh, then try to explain.

Because, truly, it *is* a very personal matter and experience, isn't it, this faith relationship we have with Jesus? It's real. The laughter of atheists doesn't disprove it; in fact, the categorical dismissal of what billions say they have experienced is both arrogant and exactly the kind of intolerance of which they so often accuse Christians.

Our faith might be dim at times or intermittent; the relationship might be shallower than we'd like it to be; we might struggle with far too many moments of doubt and enjoy too few of transcendent clarity—but whatever the character and challenges of *my* experience of God, it is my own. Nobody else, I'm sure, experiences God in exactly the same way as I do or as you do.

It makes some sense, then, that we so instinctively resist tagging our individual spiritual actualities with the one-size-fits-all label of "religion." We don't want to align ourselves with the weird public twitches and screwball attitudes of the lumbering beast with the bull's-eye on its back. And we don't want to take that precious, personal sense of connection and lock it up in the kind of inflexible box that the word has come to imply to us.

Still, I sometimes feel—maybe it's the same for you—a bit disloyal when I distance myself from the idea of religion or being religious. It's as if I'm a teenager trying to avoid being seen with a younger, socially awkward sibling. I have the niggling sense that, while I'm trying to claim something precious and powerful by focusing on the "personal relationship" bit, I'm also, just maybe, losing something by denying that I'm religious.

One way or another, we all act out publicly what we believe internally, even if our actions are sometimes unconsciously connected to our beliefs. We live our beliefs. We recycle because we believe the environment is under stress, or we toss an empty coffee cup out of the car window because we don't. We think guns facilitate violence and therefore refuse to own them, or we stockpile them because we believe the only answer to violence is more guns. We think that the truth is important and do our best to be truthful, or we believe that a few lies that deliver the desired result are justified.

Actually, we don't mind claiming this kind of integration of what we believe with how we act. In fact, we don't think much of people who claim to believe a certain way but behave contrary to those beliefs, whether they're Christians, atheists, Hindus, or politicians.

And that, I think, is the nut of our instinctive objection to religion: So many people and institutions appear to behave contrary to what they say they believe, or have beliefs that encourage destructive actions, that we don't want to be associated with that abusiveness or lack of integrity. We've come to view religion as the mindless adherence to a rigid system of behavior that at best is repressive and at worst gives issue to a wide range of dysfunctional and even vile activities. On a more mundane level, maybe we just don't want to be typecast or have our choices and activities restricted by inconvenient dogma.

Our problem, then, is not religion per se; it's *bad* religion. Sick religion, religion that the biblical writer James calls "worthless."[1]

There's no doubt that religion in general has acquired a bad name in our contemporary first-world society, and there can be little doubt that the name has been well earned. So much so that a great many of us have come to believe that all religion is the empty, worthless kind. But it's the Christian faith specifically, and the religious expression of it, that concerns you and me, so it might be helpful for us to do a little thinking about how we've arrived at the point where we often want to disown our own religion.

As Alan Hirsch points out in his insightful book *The Forgotten Ways*, the early period of the church's existence was a time of exponential growth. From the death of Christ until about AD 100, it grew from a couple hundred uncertain followers to perhaps twenty-five thousand; over the next two hundred years (by AD 310) there were as many as twenty million disciples spread throughout the world—disciples who were poor, rejected, and often actively persecuted.[2] They were proclaiming and living a religion that had integrity with the words and life of Jesus, as well as claiming for themselves the power of his death and resurrection.

Fast-forward seven or eight hundred years, and we see something quite different. The poor, weak church—that had spread throughout the Roman and Byzantine world, like yeast through a batch of dough—had become a powerful entity whose political, economic, and military might dominated the Western world. The popes maintained armies of their own, and they manipulated most of the armies of Europe by means of the sale of indulgences and threats of excommunication (the classic carrot and stick). They also crowned kings and exacted tribute from them.

And the church taught that there was no salvation except through its own offices—an individual could not approach God to confess and receive forgiveness for his or her sins; instead he or she had to do so through the seven sacraments of the church. People's souls were held, quite literally, ransom. Paying money to the church could cut years, centuries, or even millennia off the "refining" torture people would supposedly endure in purgatory before being admitted to heaven unless, if they failed the test, they were cast into hell.

The slaughter of thousands was justified during the Crusades simply because these people weren't Christians.[3] By means of the Inquisition, the church tortured and often put people to death merely because they were suspected of not being Christians or because they held divergent views on some arcane point of doctrine. During one shameful era in Spain, to be a Jew who had not publicly converted to Christianity meant certain torture and death. Even among "the faithful," people who were too poor to pay for church rites or too weak to perform the prescribed penances were (according to church doctrine) abandoned to the flames of hell.

It was such dissonance with Jesus' original teaching and way of life—which valued people who were as unlovely as a leper, as useless as a paralyzed man, as repugnantly "other" as an Ethiopian eunuch, as sinful as a prostitute, and as dangerous as a bandit or Roman centurion—that prompted the Reformation.

The Christian religion—the way people were living out what they *really* believed, as opposed to what Jesus, their putative "Lord," had taught—had made a sad, often obscene, frequently abusive caricature of the church.

Those of us who are Protestant can't afford to simply lay such bad religion at the door of our Catholic brothers and sisters. Martin Luther himself, famously and tragically, turned to virulent anti-Semitism toward the end of his life, publishing a

sixty-five-thousand-word treatise (longer than this book) titled
On the Jews and Their Lies. He proclaimed that their houses
and synagogues should be destroyed and that they were not
God's chosen nation, but the devil's people. Certainly not a
welcome to a people who were mostly poor and oppressed.

"We are at fault," he ranted, "in not slaying them."[4]

Are you groaning yet? Within a couple of decades, depending on who was on the throne, Catholics and Protestants were
taking turns torturing, decapitating, and burning one another
at the stake in England. Who in their right mind wants to be
associated with such vile lunacy?

We could work our way through the centuries from then
until now, but it would be too depressing, and most of us are
aware of these travesties already. It should be said, however,
that Christianity *has* produced much that is truly wonderful
and worth celebrating. Has anyone noticed that it's the countries with a Christian heritage in which women are most valued; tolerance of divergent political or religious views is most
practiced; freedom of speech, movement, and assembly is most
in evidence; and educational and employment opportunities
are most widely extended? Ignatius, Teresa of Ávila, Julian
of Norwich, and a slew of others who were among the greatest spiritual writers in history lived during those wicked pre-
Reformation times! Saint Francis of Assisi led a movement of
believers who took a vow of poverty, eschewed worldly power,
and dedicated themselves to announcing God's forgiveness to
all. Francis even tried, it is said, to end the Crusades. Literacy,
libraries, universities, hospitals, and nursing were all gifts of
the medieval church to European society.

Despite these bright spots, there's no doubt our failures have often been lurid and wrought on an extravagant scale. Unfortunately, the disconnect between the Good News that Jesus announced and the way we, his followers, behave is still disturbingly evident today. The church's historic addictions to money and power seem to continue. So, yes, bad religion. (Other religions have been as bad or worse.)

Although there are significant exceptions, Western Christians as a group are among the world's wealthiest people. In itself, there's nothing wrong with that, but we do tend to use our wealth to ensure that we will stay wealthy and get wealthier instead of using it to lift others out of poverty. We'll go to war to ensure that we continue to have access to a supply of cheap gasoline, and we swallow gratefully the lies we are fed that allow us to pretend there's another, more noble reason. We've shown we're willing to line up behind leaders who flog fear, hatred, bigotry, misogyny, and the other toxic symptoms of entitlement as long as we think they'll protect our hegemony and grant us the illusion of access to power. We're more interested, it seems, in worldly power than in spiritual power.

Muslim people around the world consider the wars in Iraq and Afghanistan to be religious conflicts, and they believe that Christians have invaded their countries and killed their people primarily because they are not Christian. We may not think of it that way, but *they* certainly do, and no wonder. Those wars could not have been joined by Western governments without the vocal and enthusiastic support of Western Christians.[5]

We have majored on a few issues of public morality, such as abortion and same-gender marriage, and largely abandoned the cause of biblical justice—so much so that the very word *justice* has come to mean little more in our society than state-sanctioned vengeance. We're viewed as being more concerned about same-gender marriage than we are about almost a quarter of our children who are growing up in poverty,[6] or the insanely high incarceration rates of African Americans in the States[7] and the First Nations people in Canada.[8]

Christian churches in Canada, the States, and Australia have colluded with governments, courts, and police to strip aboriginal people of their land, livelihood, freedom of movement, culture, and even children. It has been pointed out that this amounts to cultural genocide. Several of our largest denominations participated in this spiritual and economic rape of entire peoples, often adding the actual rape of children to the long black tally of our sins. We did this over a period of about one hundred and fifty years and now spend enormous amounts of money and energy trying to avoid or minimize accountability.[9]

White evangelical churches in the American South were bastions of racism and oppression through the same time period. Some, alas, still are. It's true that Christians in Britain and, later, America were at the forefront of the antislavery movement. And there are some white or mixed congregations now that are powerful advocates for the true equality of black people, but it would be hard to argue that we're leading the charge. For the most part, those of us who are white, wealthy, and Christian not only have been content to live in the privilege afforded to us by the historic oppression of aboriginal and African people, but we also do everything we can to guard that privilege as if it were a right.

On a more prosaic level, why is it that the politician who gets caught with his pants around his ankles is so often a sanctimonious, family-values, God-fearing loudmouth? Why do street preachers, who are supposedly announcing *good* news, seem so angry all the time? How, when Jesus went out of his way to heal lepers, can we resent and even obstruct providing access to health care for people who are poor? How come, when a pastor goes on TV to debate almost anything with almost anybody, he usually comes off sounding judgmental, wishy-washy, or just, well, not very bright? How do some of the most ridiculously reprehensible athletes, actors, and musicians get away with ascribing their success to God?

Whew. And that's not even taking into account the pettier inconsistencies of "believers" who make nice on Sunday and screw everyone they can through the week, or say truly hateful things about gay people and just about anybody else who is not them, or beat their wives, cheat on their taxes, insist on their right to destroy the environment, or get far more excited about football or hockey or basketball than they do about anything, *anything* that has to do with God. Plus, there's insipid worship music and lame preaching . . .

Aaaargh!

If this is religion, leave me out.

———————

A month and a half before my visit to Mike and the boys, I'd been woken by my phone vibrating on the bedside table.

"Mike calling," the display told me, and it was 4:30 a.m. This couldn't be good.

I answered, but he wasn't talking to me. *Maybe he pocket dialed me*, I thought. I could hear him at some distance from the phone, yelling at someone: "I'm here. I'm right here!" I called out to him a few times, but there was no response, and about thirty seconds later the line went dead.

"Who was it?" my wife asked blearily. "Poor Mike," Maggie said, sighing, when I told her. I called back a couple of times and got no answer, so I left a message asking him to call me as soon as he could. I was worried about him, and with good cause, as it turned out.

Later that morning, friends discovered his cryptic Facebook posts about some kind of altercation, and a photo taken from the window of his apartment of police cars and an Emergency Task Force van in the parking lot below. The caption read, "These are for me."

There had been lots of bad times, but the recent years had been mostly good. He'd found housing, had long periods of sobriety punctuated by occasional short bursts of drug use (the opposite of his former pattern), and gotten himself a little dog who became his pride and joy. He was a big presence in our worshiping community, often giving voice to thoughts and concerns with an honest vulnerability few could match. Even the news that he had stage IV cirrhosis didn't throw him too much off stride. His liver had dried up like a nut, leaving it about only 10 percent functional. But his faith stayed strong and his attitude positive. He joined a hepatitis C support group and spoke often about how great his new friends were there.

Still, the successive failures of some treatments and dis-
qualifications from others took their toll. He knew the clock
was ticking. As the disappointments mounted, he began to
"chip"—returning to his former poisons when the darkness
seemed too great to bear. As is inevitable, the sober periods
began to shorten. His behavior became increasingly volatile,
and a conflict with a couple of dealers who lived in the same
apartment building finally flipped the switch. A neighbor
claimed to have witnessed him battering his door with an ax
and shouting threats in the middle of the night.

It hadn't been easy to get him out on bail. Years before,
Mike had lived with me for several months, but that wasn't
going to work this time. He couldn't go home, and there
seemed to be nowhere else we could find him the "residential
surety" required by the court—a place to live, and someone
else living there who could be his surety.

It was Danny, Bear, and the other Mike—Mike Megna—
who stepped up. Jones House, a Sanctuary-facilitated home
they shared together, had a vacant bedroom. Long-time members of the Sanctuary community, Danny and Bear both had
lengthy rap sheets, but Megna, we were all a little shocked
to discover, had no criminal record at all! That's rare in our
patch. I put up the money, and Megna signed off as the critical
residential surety.

It was a big deal for Mike Megna, and who could blame
him? Mike had welcomed Megna to the community a couple
of years earlier, and Megna liked the guy, but he'd had no
idea he could get violent like that. Nobody really knew what
kind of state Mike would be in when he was released, and he

clearly hadn't been in a positive frame of mind when he was arrested. Megna worried that Mike might lose it again and that he, Megna, would be responsible for posting his bail—how would Mike respond to *that* if it happened? What would the courts do to Megna if he was unable to supervise Mike the way he had promised?

Bear and Danny wanted to make it clear that Mike was coming as a guest, for a couple of months if necessary, not as a prospective resident of the house. They wanted to support their brother but wisely knew the personality mix wouldn't work long term, and I agreed. They knew that, for as long as Mike stayed, there would be inevitable friction for all involved—the kind of friction that can be dangerous to the fragile stability of people who have battled addictions and long periods of homelessness for most of their adult lives.

But they counted the cost, the three of them, and then they stepped up. This is what love looks like: You lay down your life for your brother.[10]

POWER, MONEY, AND DRY BONES

Anyone who has traveled at all in European cities has seen and marveled at medieval churches, especially the magnificent cathedrals. Soaring spires that were, at the time, the tallest buildings in the world, visible for miles around; flying buttresses with incredible carvings of saints and gargoyles; tall, slender columns so delicate that they sometimes seem to hang from vaulted ceilings (their arches leaping away from the eye of the viewer far below) instead of supporting them;

stained glass with colors so rich and designs so intricate that they can hardly be replicated today; roods, choir screens, statuary, and altars, fabulous in detail and depth, wrought in metal, wood, or stone; frescoes, paintings, and tapestries—and much, much more.

I love those churches, especially the smaller ones in little towns. And I love the art, the craftsmanship, the passion for God that compelled the artisans who built them. In this way, they're a kind of redemption of the twisted motivations of the often power-drunk church leaders who ordered their construction. That's true religion.

However. They also provide a terrifically accurate illustration of the problem we face—the problem of bad religion.

The Cathedral of Saint Domnius in Split, Croatia, is one of the oldest church buildings in the world. Originally constructed around AD 300 to serve as the tomb of the Roman emperor, Diocletian, it didn't actually become a church until sometime in the sixth or seventh century, long after the fall of Rome. Diocletian had persecuted Christians, and therefore his remains were removed and disposed of ignominiously; the bones of Saint Domnius, whom he had beheaded, were interred instead.

The cathedral is small and quite modest by comparison to most in Europe, and it's an unusual hexagonal shape. Still, you can identify it immediately as a church by its tall and beautiful steeple tower, added in the late Middle Ages. Visitors pay a fee to enter and view its spectacular collection of art and carvings, including portraits of Roman persecutors of the church made back when Christian baiting was an honorable profession. For an extra five kuna, you may ascend a narrow set of stairs and view selected items from what a hand-lettered sign describes as "The Treasure of the Church."

This treasure is a collection of brocaded surplices seven or eight hundred years old, jeweled crosses, miters, chalices, staffs of silver and gold, extravagantly bound Bibles, and elaborate reliquaries containing—often displaying—the bones of saints, gray with age. Even skulls, encased in silver.

It's fabulous stuff, though a little grisly. Of course, no self-respecting medieval church is without such a treasury, and most are far "richer" than that of Saint Domnius.

But wait a second. *That's* the treasure of the church?

Soaring spires and mighty buttresses. Gold and silver. Relics of dead saints.

Power, money, and dry bones.

That, it seems to me, sums up what the critics—including many of us followers of Jesus—think of when we hear the word *religion*. Power, money, and dry bones. Unfortunately, those terms apply just as accurately to much of the church's apparent value system today, even if our architecture is less extravagant. If that's what we're repudiating, we're right to do so.

Domnius and the other martyrs whose bones were dug up and delivered to the cathedral, long after their deaths, were people who had lived and laid down their lives in the most radical fashion because they loved and followed Jesus. They did not suck up to worldly power or pursue material goods. They did not seek to dominate others or create an artificial means of controlling the access of others to God's Kingdom. Neither did they live a private, individualized faith. They didn't major in the minor aspects of Christian dogma, point an accusing finger at the morality of others, or claim that their parishioners *expected* them to drive a gold-plated chariot.

Instead, they boldly announced that Jesus—not the Roman emperor—was King of kings and deserved their complete allegiance. They welcomed the people whom everyone else had rejected, insisting that salvation and God's grace was for everyone—especially the poor. They preached that this salvation was free, that no one could stand between God and another human being. They fed the hungry, shared what they had with people in need, and called it an act of worship. They said that Jesus was God, not the pantheon of Rome or Caesar. They claimed that no act of man was so vile that it was beyond forgiveness, that God alone is judge. They did battle with the powers of their present world and knew that, in dying, they had not lost.

I hope that God, in his mercy, prevents those old saints from seeing what has been done with their bones. I think that, even in heaven, it would cause them to weep.

Mike's friends had been aching for him for a year or more already. He'd taken hit after hit: The failure of a six-month chemo-style treatment that was supposed to cure his hepatitis C but instead left him weak, wasted, and emotionally spun; his diagnosis with final-stage cirrhosis; a period when his public-housing apartment became unlivable; his disqualification from further hep C treatment programs; the fear, anger, and confusion he felt at having been trapped and pistol-whipped during a convenience-store robbery he happened into; the heartbreak with the son and daughter with whom he'd worked so hard to reconnect and reconcile; his increasingly frequent battles with the drugs he had once appeared to have largely beaten.

And then it got worse.

Mike Megna went with him to the appointment and so did Paula, Mike's hep C support worker. I was there, too, when the possibility we had avoided talking about was confirmed. Cancer.

"Months," said the doctor, in answer to the impossible question. Then, after a pause, "Not a year."

———————

And so now here is Mike, sitting in a plastic chair at the end of the porch a couple of weeks before Christmas. His mind is whirling with fear and anger and sorrow, and as it whirls, it flings bitterness from his mouth. It's the comprehensively tragic scope of Mike's life that ratifies for me the heroic nature of his faith. Later, I will complain to my wife, "He's been screwed since the moment he was born! Why can't God at least give him a break? This is just so not fair." If anyone I know has grounds to curse God and die, it's my brother Mike.

But I do know my brother. He discovered long ago where his only real hope lies, and he knows that hope will never let go of him, nor will he let go of it. It's not easy to remember this, or trust it entirely, in this particular moment. Everybody's emotions are high, the situation precarious. Mike is lost in his anger and bitter disappointment—at God, life, his friends, himself. The instinct in all of us to meet aggression with aggression is very lively, and no one even seems quite sure exactly where it started.

Greg Cook, another member of the Sanctuary community, arrives and sidles quietly up onto the porch. A good and trusted friend to each of the people living here, he says little, being unsure of how the situation has evolved and where it stands, but his calmness radiates.

The door opens, and Danny steps out. The tension rises again. He stands there for a beat or two, hands in the pockets of the hooded sweatshirt he has slipped on.

"Mike," he says. "I love you, brother. I want you to stay. We all screw up. I screw up. I want you to stay."

And the hard mask of anger Mike has been wearing slips, then melts entirely. He weeps—his chest and shoulders heaving.

Now Megna slips onto the porch, slides past Danny, and plants himself in a chair he has hiked as close as possible to Mike. Christian faith and this crazy, capricious street culture are both relatively new to him, too, and I know he finds it a little like camping on the lip of an active volcano.

He reaches out and clutches the hand lying limp on Mike's knee.

"I want to pray for you," he says. And he does. Beautiful, simple, broken stuff.

In the silence that follows, Mike takes the cigarette Danny

extends to him, takes this peace offering and lights it, and the smoke, I think, ascends to the nostrils of God.

———————

The Jones House boys held Mike until the courts allowed him to return home. Megna attended each of Mike's court appearances and most of his doctor's appointments with him. Days later, Megna told me that his experience that night was a revelation to him—he'd seen God in action in a way that he had never known before, and he was hungry for more of it.

Driving home that night, I marveled too, at the true religion I had witnessed—a real, functioning body, flesh and bone, muscular with grace and love.

While writing this story, my own emotions caught up with me, and I had to stop for a while. I sent a text message to Mike:

I've been writing about you again today, and weeping. You're a hero of the faith to me. I love you.[11]

Mike responded:

I love you to Greg its all good Lord know best. Big Hug … now get back to writing.[12]

spiritual or religious?

I HAD JUST PLACED my open Bible on our wobbly old Communion table and was opening my mouth to speak, when a racket in the main entrance stairwell interrupted me. None of our group of fifty or so could see what was happening at first, but we could hear it: the door banging open, slamming shut; the steel nosings on the stairs clattering wildly; a woman's voice leading the way, shrieking panicked profanities; the door banging open again, followed by a man shouting more of the same.

Abandoning my place near the middle of the room—our worship, Communion, and teaching takes place "in the round," as the theater people say—I stepped around the table and began to move toward the entrance of the little auditorium. A few others began to stand up, wondering what to do next. We barely had time to move when Robyn burst into the room, cradling one arm with the other and running as fast as she could.

Robyn was sobbing and flinging incoherent curses over her shoulder. I spread my arms a bit in a "what on earth do you think you're doing?" kind of gesture. Robyn opened hers, too, and ran right into me. She squeezed me fiercely, hanging on as if I were a log in a raging river, and my arms instinctively closed around her.

I had an inkling who might momentarily follow her through the door, and sure enough, here he came, spitting invective, snorting mightily, and practically pawing the ground. Others had moved to stand quietly between us. He skidded to a halt, realizing he'd come as far as he could. The shift within him from blind rage to bluster was actually visible.

"Darren," I called across the human barrier. "Go. Go now." He was a short plug of a man, tattooed to the knuckles—not with the clever, colorful sleeves of a hipster but with the blurred, blue-green phantasms of the jailhouse—and had pale scars snaking through the dark stubble on his head. After lobbing a few more threats and insults, with decreasing vigor, he turned and swaggered out.

IT'S TEMPTING, BUT . . .

Given the travesties the church has committed in the past and the nonsense it still gets stuck in today, it's tempting to just chuck the whole notion of religion into the waste bin of failed concepts.

Mighty tempting, indeed. Especially when we ourselves are also guilty of many of those inconsistencies.

Millions upon millions of people are doing just that—chucking religion. How often have you heard this one: "I'm spiritual but not religious"? That's a relatively new concept. I'm sure I never heard a statement like that during my high school years or anytime soon after, but it's becoming very common.

Consider this:

> The number of Americans who do not identify with
> any religion also has grown in recent years; indeed,
> about one-fifth of the public overall—and a third
> of adults under age 30—are religiously unaffiliated
> as of 2012. Fully a third of U.S. adults say they do
> not consider themselves a "religious person." And
> two-thirds of Americans—affiliated and unaffiliated
> alike—say religion is losing its influence in
> Americans' lives.[1]

Those numbers are even higher in Canada, with a National Household Survey reporting that almost a quarter of Canadian residents have no religious affiliation at all[2]—a figure that has risen by about 8 percent in the past decade. It's about the same in the UK.[3]

Even within the majority who still identify as Christian, a significant shift is apparent. George Barna, a researcher who has specialized in analyzing religious and spiritual trends for many years, observes the following:

While more than two-thirds of Americans say they are either "religious" or "spiritual," they admit to not being deeply committed to faith matters. Fewer than one in five (18%) claims to be "totally committed" to engaging in personal spiritual development. Further evidence shows that among adults who claim to be Christian, just one out of every seven (14%) say that their faith in and relationship with God is the highest priority in their life.[4]

Among younger people, the shift is even more stark. For eighteen- to twenty-nine-year-olds who grew up regularly attending church, almost 60 percent have quit going.[5] In other words, we're not connecting what we say we believe to what happens in church. Or we're chucking the beliefs entirely.

Still, people cling to the idea of being spiritual, even if they're not interested in formal religion. I know atheists and agnostics who are deeply, genuinely interested in spirituality. I know Christians who feel that going to church is actually an impediment to their spiritual growth.

Religion, as we understand it, is becoming less and less valid to us, but our hunger for real, deep, sustaining, and refreshing spirituality is as voracious as ever.

People who profess a nonreligious spirituality might say that they encounter the spiritual when they encounter mystery, when they are struck emotionally by the beauty of a sunset or experience a moment that is, for reasons that remain obscure, transcendent. Wonder has a lot to do with it.

Often, such people are particularly sensitive to the essential fraternity of humanity and the magnificence of the natural world. Fragility touches them. Creativity moves them. They tend to be curious and want to be open to possibilities that others might consider absurd or valueless. They believe that the universe is made of more than atoms and molecules and that life of any sort is precious.

While the sacraments of baptism and Communion may have no value to them, eating a square of chocolate (dark, probably—antioxidants and all that) or paddling a canoe along the shore of a quiet lake would seem to them like much the same thing.

They don't want to be bound by rules that don't make sense to them and are set for them by someone else. They want to be free.

To such folk, and such values, I utter a quiet "Amen." Except, of course, that baptism and Communion *do* have value to me. (Also, I prefer milk chocolate.)

As attractive as such an unfettered spirituality is, it does present some problems.

SPIRITUAL DICHOTOMY

I'd suggest that there's another side to what a lot of people really mean when they say, "I'm spiritual but not religious" or even more so, "My spirituality is very private." I think what many people really mean is "I don't want you talking to me about it. I don't want people scrutinizing my faith, because if they do, I'll have to scrutinize it, too—and I may discover that my spirituality isn't all that deep or coherent or integrated with the way I really live. Furthermore, if I have to start actually declaring what I believe, I'll be held accountable by what I say—I'll have to actually behave accordingly."

And there's the rub. As much as we might like to at times, we can't divorce our inner, individual, spiritual lives from our outer, communal, material lives. When we try to do so, or actually do separate what we say we believe from how we live day to day, we do violence to both ourselves and our society. We dichotomize our own souls.

Those four out of five Christians identified by Barna as admitting that they aren't really deeply committed to their faith are living with a destructive dissonance at the very heart of their lives. By distancing themselves from whatever they find demanding or contradictory about the tenets of their religion, they are cutting themselves off not only from the benefits of it but also, in some measure, from their sense of identity as the people of God.

It's understandable, but it's tragic.

This kind of gap can lead to us succumbing, usually in simple ways, to the blandishments of the culture around us. When our actions don't line up with our beliefs, we begin to feel shame about those inconsistencies, and that starts a destructive cycle. We isolate ourselves more from the people around us for whom the church thing seems to work—and it does seem to work for some, doesn't it?—and then we feel guilty about that, too.

All those well-ordered lives and those shiny faces, brightly turned toward the pastor on Sunday morning. *It must work for them; it just doesn't work for me,* is how our thinking goes, *and that means there must be something wrong with me. I don't trust enough, read Scripture enough, pray enough . . . the Bible study group is boring, and even when the preacher is lights-out good, I can't remember what he said three days later.*

Seriously, how many times have you listened to a sermon that significantly changed your life? Once? Twice? Never?

Listen, I preach a lot—at Sanctuary, other churches, and conferences. Let me tell you a secret: It's not working very well for most of the shiny-faced folk either. As a visiting speaker— a stranger—I routinely have people tell me something that they feel they can't share with anyone in the church. Those bright eyes and big smiles are often hiding the same kind of disappointment and resignation that you and I so often feel.

It's clear, if you read through the Barna material, that the majority of Christians are pretty dissatisfied with their spiritual lives. Maybe they avoid deep commitment simply because it's inconvenient and less entertaining than movies or March Madness. Or because of that desire to be free from the expectations of others. Or they've tried the Bible studies and small groups, and they didn't work. But maybe it's because what they are being asked to commit themselves to doesn't ring true or isn't challenging or fulfilling enough.

Here's what conventional church provides us: some instruction in what the Bible says and how that should affect our lives; some cool and entertaining stuff for the kiddies, so they don't go looking for trouble; some rituals that either comfort us or ratify some of life's big events; a handful of people who will pray for us, if things are going so badly that we become desperate enough to submit the bare facts for publication in the church bulletin; a group of people who remind us that we are not alone in believing this wild story about God becoming a man, and so on; the occasional opportunity to do something good (but simple, not too demanding) for people elsewhere who are struggling; a little inspiration once in a while, if we're lucky.

In our guts, we know that this is not all the church is supposed to be.

Although their relationship was relatively new, I'd known both Darren and Robyn[6] for years. He had been an important figure in Sanctuary's early days, quite involved in community life, and even a kind of prophetic voice from the streets as to what we needed to become together. The combined weight of his early life traumas and the addictions, homelessness, and criminal behaviors—and further traumas prompted by these—had taken their toll. For some time he'd been unable to be present in our community without becoming violent. And although this required that we bar him for the safety of others, several of us still made efforts to stay connected with him on the streets.

Robyn had never, as far as I can remember, attended a Sunday worship gathering before. Darren had. But I'm sure she didn't think of herself as a member of the Sanctuary church. She came because of the connection she had found—and the relationships that had grown—through years of partaking of our community meals throughout the week, attending a drop-in for women only (exclusive precisely because of the kind of thing she had experienced that day with Darren), and receiving health care in our little clinic from nurses she knew not only as health care professionals but also as friends. She had often chatted with our outreach teams and other community members on the street, and she'd received help with social service conflicts, support when she wanted to visit her parents out of town, and warm clothing in cold weather. Practical things that, added up, were the currency of simple human friendship. She had sat in drop-ins and talked with any number of us about any number of things, serious and not so serious, as friends do.

The archetypal background of a street-involved woman is this: a victim of early life trauma (likely including sexual abuse), which can lead to addictions, more traumas, street involvement, periods of homelessness, and of course abusive relationships with a succession of men all throughout. It seemed likely that Robyn's history mirrored much of this distressingly common pattern.

It turned out Darren had already broken her wrist somewhere out on the street before she wrenched free of him and ran blindly, instinctively, to the only safe place she knew. Someone in our gathering had called the cops, and they responded with commendable alacrity.

The female officer who interviewed Robyn was compassionate, patient, and respectful. After making sure that Robyn was safe with the officer and a couple of other women from our community, I finally returned to the members of our worshiping community, who had been waiting patiently and prayerfully throughout.

We're used to interruption in our Sunday gatherings. Our group, though small, is amazingly diverse—homeless men and women, university and seminary students, people whose addictions are still active and others who are in recovery, young professionals and social workers, a mix of ethnicities, and even a handful of middle-aged, middle-class "normal" folks. On any given Sunday, we're likely to have someone hijack our time together with a psychotic rant, drunken jokes or anger, inappropriate song requests, or the uncensored expression of a soul made raw by anguish.

And we've come to realize that, very often, we're not being "hijacked" after all. Sometimes the interruption proves to be the action and even voice of the Spirit of God. I'm invited to speak every now and then in large churches where the Sunday service is a carefully orchestrated production, timed to the minute. At Sanctuary, not infrequently, something comes off the rails even before we've begun.

So although it's not generally as dramatic as Darren chasing Robyn into the sanctuary, and although the police don't usually attend, we're used to strange and even upsetting things happening. I don't imagine I was the only one thinking, once the initial excitement had abated, *What is God showing us here?*

THE GOSPEL HAS TWO SHOES

Have you ever had a real encounter with God? I bet you have. Maybe several. Such encounters, even among people who are not particularly religious, are encouragingly common. But not many of those encounters seem to take place when we are sitting in a church service. They tend to happen when we are out in the world, involved in real life. That alone is worth reflecting on.

No wonder we tend to hang on to the religious aspects of our faith out of a sense of duty, rather than living them enthusiastically because they set our hearts on fire.

As hard as it may seem that I'm being on our typical experience of church, I don't think it's the essential problem. It's the symptom, not the disease. The church herself—the body of Christ in our groaning world and his bride in the one to come—is powerful and beautiful, a mighty, transcendent army whose weapons are faith, hope, and love, marching through the ages and into eternity. When she sings, the angels bow their heads in awe; healing is in her hands, and her feet are shod with the gospel.[7]

The gospel of Jesus Christ is what we're supposed to stand and march on. But wait, one of her shoes is missing . . .

How would you describe that gospel? Would it be something like this? "Jesus of Nazareth was and is God incarnate. He died and rose again to save us, and all who put their trust in him can be sure of forgiveness, cleansing, and eternal life with God."

I believe all of that. It's my only hope, and it fills me with gratitude. If I didn't believe this, I doubt I'd be much interested in God. Instead, my energies would go into pleasing myself as much as possible. I do believe.

But it's only one shoe.

Depending on what Christian tradition you hail from,

you may add a phrase or two to my summation of the gospel above, but this is the core of what most people who call themselves Christians believe. This is the gospel that evangelicals, in particular, have stressed for generations.

The problem with this summation is that it is only about me. My salvation. My relationship with Jesus Christ. My confidence of forgiveness, God's interest in me, my progressive sanctification, and one day, my eternal life. It's me and Jesus, just the two of us. Oh, I may—and I should—offer it to other people too, but they will experience it in the same individual, private manner that I do.

The practical problem with this individuation is that it places us in a kind of holy quarantine. We have little sense of a communal gospel—that is, a life in which we are working out our salvation together with others.[8] There is no inherent obligation to the world around us. There is not even a real sense of obligation to the community of believers.

Most of us go to church as consumers, not communers. We receive the service being provided and leave. We have little sense of living out the gospel together, day by day, in the world. Our souls struggle on in a spiritual vacuum that renders those experiences we do share rote, unreal, or superficial.

Luke described the early church like this: "All the believers were one in heart and mind. No one claimed that any of their possessions was their own, but they shared everything they had."[9] Not many of us experience anything even close to that with other believers.

The theological fault to which our typical experience of church bears witness is a partial gospel. A truncated, one-shoe gospel, hopping awkwardly along. A gospel that is only about the salvation of individuals minimizes the greater truth that Christ was crucified and resurrected to reconcile *all things* to himself and to defeat *all forms* of sin and death. As the apostle Paul put it,

> The creation was subjected to futility, not willingly,
> but because of him who subjected it, in hope that
> the creation itself will be set free from its bondage to
> corruption and obtain the freedom of the glory of the
> children of God. For we know that the whole creation
> has been groaning together in the pains of childbirth
> until now.[10]

The gospel that Jesus announced and lived was not only about rescuing and healing individuals; it was also about dismantling the oppressive systems of the world—spiritual, religious, political, economic, cultural, and so on—and reconciling "to himself all things, whether on earth or in heaven, making peace by the blood of his cross."[11]

What this means is that when Jesus said he had been "anointed . . . to proclaim good news to the poor,"[12] he meant just that. He meant that setting people free from the oppression of poverty, and from the systems and conditions that keep them poor, is just as much gospel as setting them free from the spiritual oppression of sin.

That's the other shoe. The gospel needs both in order to walk.

Some call this "social justice" and see it as antithetical to the announcing of the gospel of personal salvation. They think it's tantamount to preaching that performing good works will save you. They forget that this is part of both Jesus' teaching and his work of reconciliation, that this is *biblical* or *Kingdom* justice: a much livelier, grander concept than social work with a spiritual gloss. A justice that is only social is a meager thing by comparison, impoverished in the articles of imagination, spiritual vitality, and deep human connection.

Others see caring for the poor as one of many possible legitimate activities in which the church or a Christian individual may be engaged, but they still regard justice as distinct from the gospel—that is, separate from the work of the Cross, not an inherent part of the evangel. The gospel, for them, is only about the salvation of individuals, and Kingdom justice is an elective. Such a gospel shortchanges the work of Christ and the power of the Cross and the Resurrection.

The pre-Reformation church also proclaimed a truncated gospel, one in which submission to the church replaced simple faith in Christ as the means of salvation. It seems that the evil one has devised an enduring and effective strategy to cripple the church: Divide the gospel into bits so that Christians will be inclined to embrace and defend their own little bits—often from one another!—instead of the whole.

A partial gospel results in an empty religion. We end up with either a privatized, individualized spirituality that never quite walks in the real world or a set of obligations and activities that aren't animated by a lively Spirit. In both cases, we end up hopping along on one foot.

Taking the wonderful truth that God has saved you through

the work of Christ and stashing it in some internal vault to be cashed in after you die is a dismal, impoverished way to live. So is going through the motions of religious observation that are sectioned off from your daily reality.

Spiritual or religious? It's not a matter of choosing between them. We need to be both. I don't mean we *should* be both. I mean we *need* to be.

That's true spirituality and true religion.

———————————

"I don't think there's much point in going on with our usual teaching time," I said to the group once things had calmed down. "I know what the passage is because my Bible is still open to it here on the table, but I haven't got a clue now what I was going to say. Besides, I think it's pretty clear that God has already spoken to us."

An object lesson is a powerful teaching tool—and even more so if you're the object.

A financially poor, physically and emotionally abused woman—the very icon of an oppressed person—had fled her oppressor and run directly into the arms of "the church." It could hardly have been more literal: It was my privilege to supply the actual arms that enclosed her, but much of the congregation had instinctively surrounded us. Robyn, her wrist already fractured, and knowing that more battering was on its way, had fled to the one place and the one people she knew would put themselves between her and further harm.

Later, I wondered, *How do we also hold Darren?* Because

he, too, was clearly one of "the prisoners" to whom Jesus had come to proclaim freedom.[13] And I realized that we had instinctively been trying to do that, too. Far from perfectly, but certainly consistently, over almost twenty years. He'd been not much more than a street kid when I first met him. He'd been in and out of jail, through short periods of sobriety and long periods of substance abuse, housed and homeless, and although there had been long stretches when he was so out of control we couldn't afford to let him in the building, we had maintained some kind of relationship with him. Still cared. And despite his performance that day, I'm pretty sure he knew that.

"Isn't this exactly who we're supposed to be?" I asked our little gathering. "Hasn't God been teaching us tonight what the church, the body of Christ, is supposed to do? Open its arms to the one who is frightened, broken, oppressed, and hold her right at the center?"

(FAITH = RESTING) + (RELIGION = WORKING)

Faith in God—the inner spirituality we've been talking about—isn't about doing good works. We can't work our way to believing in him or trusting that things are good between us. We can't work our way to peace. We're sinful by nature and practice, and we can never by any amount of effort become perfect. Even if we could, there's the stuff in our past that we'd have to answer for. Nope, we're not going to be able to prove to God (we can't even prove it to ourselves!) that we're good enough to meet his standards.

All we can do is rest. Stop trying. Stop pretending. Stop attempting to prove a lie that even we don't believe. Just stop and rest. It's not about convincing ourselves that we are good enough, after all. God offers mercy and grace. Mercy only has value to the guilty, and grace can only be for the undeserving.

We rest in God because we believe and trust—we have faith—that he is big enough to carry us; gracious enough to forgive and heal us; and faithful enough to never, ever let go of us.

Religion really isn't about sitting in a church auditorium, listening to a preacher or a worship band. Not even if you stand up and wave your hands above your head. It's not about signing your name to a statement of faith, identifying yourself with a given denomination, or even calling yourself a Christian. It isn't about arguing doctrine. It isn't about us trying to reach out to God—he has already reached out to us and continues to do so every second of every day.

It isn't about toeing the line or doing what you're told, and it's not about following the rules that tell you what kind of entertainment is okay, what sort of job you can hold, how you should vote, or where you should send your kids to school.

True religion is about doing stuff that is the result of truly resting in God. We work because God is at work, and he wants us right there beside him, like children learning from a parent, doing the work he does. Because he reaches out to us when we're guilty, we look for ways to extend mercy to others who are guilty too. Because he gave us his all—Jesus—when we least deserved it, we offer grace to other people, *especially* when they don't deserve it. Because he set us free and raised us up, we look for ways to pay it forward, seeking to release others from bondage and oppression of all kinds, whether spiritual, material, or sociological. It costs something to work like this.

We do this work for the same reason that an artist paints, a surgeon operates, or a woodworker shapes a chair from raw lumber—because there's something in us that *has* to get out. If it doesn't, it will wither and die. But if it does—well, when real faith expresses itself as true religion, it's pure joy.

This sounds all wonderful and sweet, but it's not, really. It's hard. That's why it's called work.

Faith Is Private/Individual; Religion Is Public/Communal.

This is hardly news, but it has to be said: There's nobody else in the entire world, or in the history of the entire world, who is exactly like you. The details of your genetics are unique, and the sum of your experiences is unique. You see things from a perspective that no one else replicates precisely. You communicate, both sending and receiving, in a way that is so specifically and exclusively *you* that even the people closest to you are sometimes mystified by what's going on inside your head.

In this sense, our spirituality *is*, in fact, private and individual. God knows my name, and this is a source of great comfort and joy. Nobody else really fully understands the language in which God and I whisper to each other in the middle of the night.

God, however, is not selfish. He doesn't want to keep us exclusively to himself. The Trinity is the original community, the original family. We, too, made in that image, find our proper place among other people. We long to belong.

Religion is the means by which we answer that longing to find our place within the family of God. We've been made to need other people and to need being needed. Love expands—a real love in any one relationship causes us to want to reach out beyond that relationship, to extend the bounty of that love to others. Real love is never exclusive. The God who is the source of all love, who is love itself,[14] always has arms wide open.

Religion is not about everyone thinking the same way or even believing exactly the same things. *Community*, which can be interpreted as "to be one with,"[15] is not the same as *conformity*, which denotes "to be the same as."[16] Community doesn't root itself in agreement, but in love. That's why Jesus insisted that his one essential commandment was "Love one another."[17]

A faith lived in secrecy or isolation is bound to twist in on itself. It will become perverse and domineering or weak and irrelevant. A religion without room for individual, even idiosyncratic relationship with God will suffocate the very faith on which it feeds.

Faith Produces Spiritual Integrity; Religion Produces Kingdom Justice.

If our faith has any validity at all, it will shape who we are. Faith is not about giving a merely intellectual assent to a set of precepts, but embracing them with the totality of our being. It is about our spirits answering to the Spirit of God, not merely an obedience to command but the deep, instinctive yes that comes from the bottom of our souls.

We are perfectly capable of "believing" a set of facts and, at the same time, behaving contrary to them. Most of us believe that the environment is under significant stress, but in the States, each person produces approximately one ton of garbage every year.[18] We believe that certain foods are bad for us but keep scarfing them down. Some of us are even tortured by the sneaking suspicion that we just haven't been good enough to get into heaven, even though we believe in God's grace.

That's not faith. Faith is not so much about believing as it is about trusting. And when we trust God, when our spirits rest in his Spirit, he begins to change us. In fact, we can tell where faith is growing in our lives by the fruit it produces:

> The fruit of the Spirit is love, joy, peace, forbearance, kindness, goodness, faithfulness, gentleness and self-control. Against such things there is no law. . . . Since we live by the Spirit, let us keep in step with the Spirit.[19]

"Thy kingdom come," we often pray, "Thy will be done in earth, as it is in heaven."[20] We want the fruit that is growing within us to grow elsewhere and in others, too. In the Kingdom for whose advent we pray, the last shall be first, the chains of oppression are broken, afflictions are healed, childlike simplicity is a source of greatness, the prisons are opened, the hungry are fed, and those who have been rejected everywhere else are welcomed. This Kingdom belongs to people who are "poor in spirit."

In sum, it is a place where the King's justice reigns. Religion means enacting that Kingdom justice, here and now. We can't say we believe these values to be important if we are not actively living them out, together, day by day. We are the body of Christ in the world, the agents of the King.

The people whom Jesus describes as "righteous"—that is, people who enact God's justice in their relationships with other people—are ones who feed the hungry, give drink to the thirsty, welcome the stranger, clothe the naked, and visit people who are sick or in prison.[21] In doing so, these righteous ones discover that they have been caring for Christ himself.

And that righteousness equals fruitful religion, an outward expression that brings us all the way back around to a deeper, more intimate personal relationship with the one in whom our faith rests.

Real faith and true religion. Bones and muscle. A living body, opening its arms.

dry bones

THE CONNECTION between inner, individual spiritual belief and outer, communal religion—the convictions that prompt a person to act consistently in certain ways with and toward other people—is precisely what the biblical writer James tried to describe and encourage.

The James who wrote the epistle that bears his name is thought not to have been one of the Sons of Thunder—the Zebedee brothers, James and John—who seem to have been pals and fishing partners of Peter. Neither is it likely that he was James, the son of Alphaeus, another of Jesus' disciples. As with most books of the Bible, there's a considerable range of argument about who did write the book and when and where.

Most scholars go along with the earliest of the church fathers to weigh in on the matter, Origen and Eusebius, who lived about 150 years and 250 years, respectively, after the death of Jesus.

They both attributed the book to the man the apostle Paul refers to in Galatians 1:19 as "James, the Lord's brother." The biological brother of Jesus, this James was the primary leader of the church in Jerusalem. If he was, in fact, the author of this letter, it must have been among the earliest of the New Testament books to have been written, probably even before the Gospels.

James was a man who had Jewish religion in his bones, and he knew just how dry and lifeless it could become. Still, it seems that he clung doggedly to the Hebrew traditions. He didn't become a follower of his older brother until after Jesus' death—in fact, it seems it took a personal visit from the resurrected one to convince him.[1]

When we encounter him in the Acts of the Apostles or in the letters of Paul, he usually appears to be trying to steer a middle path between the law God gave to Moses and the revelations that have been coming fast and furious to the followers of Jesus—notably, Peter and Paul. He carefully compares this new perspective with Old Testament Scripture, and from the synthesis, he delivers measured direction.[2] Possibly the most conservative of the first generation of church leaders and missionaries, he understands that the Old Testament has not become worthless, but instead should form a foundation for, without constricting, this new movement of the Spirit of God.

The link between the two is his own brother, Jesus. His death and resurrection certainly changed everything, unveiling an entirely new spiritual reality, a radically different mode of relationship between God and humanity. But his life and teaching are critical elements in the link, too—the "other shoe."

I believe that James is trying to articulate what, to him and others of his era, was a new religion, the religion of Jesus—how what Jesus believed manifested itself in the way he interacted with other individuals and society at large. James is struggling to integrate what Jesus taught and how he lived into his own understanding and practice of the law. After all, Jesus had said that he hadn't come to do away with the law, but to fulfill it.[3]

"Fulfill" it? To bring to fullness or completion. What could that mean? Not the same thing as merely keeping the law, that seems clear.

Because keeping the Commandments had long since devolved into most of the things we decry as bad or false religion. Jesus had repeatedly shone a light into the cavernous warehouses of Pharisee and Sadducee religions, and he revealed that they were empty. A spiritual void. Elaborate form but no content.

Over and over, the Pharisees got all in a twist about Jesus healing people on the Sabbath. They were so bent on keeping their religious rules that they actually resented a blind man's sight being restored or a lame man's legs being straightened and strengthened. Healing someone, in their view, *was too much like work!* How blind and petty is that?

In their view, keeping the religious rules was an end in itself. So determined were they to do so that they sucked every bit of life out of the special relationship they were supposed to have with God and clean forgot that the "rules" were supposed to serve them. "The Sabbath was made for man," Jesus had to remind them, "not man for the Sabbath."[4]

The Sadducees, on the other hand, didn't care so much about behavior. It was the dogma that concerned them most.

> The Sadducees, who say there is no resurrection,
> came to him [Jesus] with a question. "Teacher," they
> said, "Moses wrote for us that if a man's brother
> dies and leaves a wife but no children, the man
> must marry the widow and raise up offspring for his
> brother. Now there were seven brothers."[5]

They went on to spin a ridiculous story about an impossibly complicated situation in an effort to prove that the concept of resurrection was itself ridiculous. What seemed to be most important to them was proving their point—being intellectually superior. Maybe there was the added bonus of knowing that if there was no resurrection, there would be no repercussions after death regarding what they chose to do in life.

Both parties, Pharisees and Sadducees—the conservatives and the liberals, you might say—were so greedy for money and power that, in the end, they were willing to lie, bribe, threaten, and murder in order to protect their hegemony.

Whatever "fulfilling the law" might mean, that definitely wasn't it.

Perhaps, in part, James was remembering the blabbermouth religiosity of those two groups when he wrote,

> Those who consider themselves religious and yet
> do not keep a tight rein on their tongues deceive
> themselves, and their religion is worthless. Religion
> that God our Father accepts as pure and faultless is
> this: to look after orphans and widows in their distress
> and to keep oneself from being polluted by the world.[6]

From chapter 4 onward, we'll begin to look in detail at the kind of integrated spiritual and religious life—faith and works—that James was trying to describe. We'll find that he gives very practical, pragmatic instruction about how to live out what Jesus taught. He certainly doesn't want it to become empty words or rote ritual, the kind of religion he describes above as "worthless." But he does want these Christians, these followers of the Way, to have some skin in the game.

But it's clear from that same passage, isn't it, that James believes true religion, religion that is "pure and faultless," is both vital and very doable? That, in fact, it's what God wants from us?

We've looked at what we understand the word *religion* to mean in contemporary terms and (perhaps reluctantly) concluded that if we are going to have a relationship with God, a spirituality that is at all real and lively, we're also going to be positively religious. That is, we're going to be engaging the world around us in a constructive, fruitful way that accurately expresses our personal relationships with God. Living out, publicly and communally, what we believe privately and individually. And when we put it like that, "religion" doesn't sound so bad!

"RELIGION" IN THE BIBLE

Oddly enough, there is no Hebrew word in the Old Testament text that corresponds exactly to our word *religion*. Of course, there are a number of other words and concepts that certainly illustrate what we mean. Those words, especially within the books detailing the Mosaic law, are used over and over. Typically, they are translated as "ordinance," "statute," or "law." So, then, the kind of thing that we religion-shy people tend to steer away from: the rules and regulations of religious observance.

Feast, or its opposite, *fast*, are two other common concepts. Feasting we get—we celebrate easily and naturally this way, and so did the Hebrew people. God, apparently, isn't against his people kicking back and having a good time. While we might list Christmas, Thanksgiving, and maybe Easter as times when we feast in religious celebration, Yahweh appointed *seven* annual national feast times. The first three were concurrent, taking place over the course of an entire week. The last, the Feast of Tabernacles, also took a week and appears to have originally been much like a massive national campout and barbecue.

Fasting, on the other hand, certainly doesn't come as easily to us. This is what people did when they were getting really serious about some great personal or national need. Not eating between sunup and sundown was intended to remind them through the course of the day to pray. In time, some people began to make a big deal of fasting as a sign of their spiritual superiority—they'd make sure everybody knew that they were fasting. Instead of cultivating humility, fasting cultivated pride. Jesus chided the Pharisees about this.[7]

God spoke to the Hebrew people about fasting in a way that made abundantly clear the difference between empty religious observance and a vital faith being lived out day by day:

On the day of your fasting [religious observance], you do
    as you please
    and exploit all your workers.
Your fasting ends in quarreling and strife . . .
You cannot fast as you do today
    and expect your voice to be heard on high.
Is this the kind of fast [religion] I have chosen,
    only a day for people to humble themselves? . . .
Is that what you call a fast,
    a day acceptable to the LORD?

Is not this the kind of fasting I have chosen:
to loose the chains of injustice
    and untie the cords of the yoke,
to set the oppressed free
    and break every yoke?
Is it not to share your food with the hungry
    and to provide the poor wanderer with shelter—
when you see the naked, to clothe them,
    and not to turn away from your own flesh and
      blood?[8]

It's abundantly clear from this passage that God's idea of meaningful religious activity was starkly different from that of the Jewish people at the time. They wanted to go to church; God wanted them to go to work. They wanted to keep everything they could for themselves; God wanted them to share what they had with the needy. They wanted to keep control; God wanted them to set people free.

It's a perfect illustration of the difference between the bad religion that makes us queasy—even if we still in some measure practice it—and the true religion that James refers to as "pure and faultless."

This passage also brings us to another Old Testament conceptualization of what we might call religion: *justice*. And justice, God's justice, is the overarching conceptualization of what true religion ought to be.

The Hebrew word *mispat*, and its variants, are usually translated as "just," "justice," and "judgment." In the Israelite context, unlike in our justice systems, this did not mean the state punishing someone for having done wrong. It was not about retribution but restoration. It meant righting wrongs that had been done, restoring what had been lost or taken away, bringing inequities in the world and communal life into line with God's standard of goodness. It meant ensuring that everyone had enough, everyone had a place where they belonged, and everyone was treated with dignity.

In a few places in the Law, the same word is used to describe the priests receiving their *due* from the people of Israel—food and other modes of support that were to be given because the priestly tribe of Levi, unlike the other tribes, was not to be granted any land for themselves.[9] They would care for the rest of the tribes spiritually, and the rest of the tribes would care for them materially.

God's justice—God's idea of real religion—is all about making sure that we're interdependent, understanding, and valuing the gifts that each one brings to the community and making sure that everyone gets what they need. This religion is not private, personal, individual. It's communal. The concept of civil rights is the shadow cast by justice, divorced as it may be from God's authority and animating vigor. As pale as civil rights may appear compared to justice, we respond instinctively to them, recognizing them as vital, precisely because they have their root in the character of the God who created us—a God whose intention is to go far beyond our *rights* and shower us with his *favor*.

As we might expect, because he was a Jewish rabbi, Jesus never used a word that could accurately be translated as "religion" either. He did, however, often speak about justice. In particular, as Paul would later, he spoke about "righteousness." Righteousness means behaving rightly toward other people: justice in the context of interpersonal relationships. In fact, in most places in the New Testament where our versions give us "righteous" or "righteousness," it should really be rendered "just" or "justice." Righteousness is living out the just character of God in our relationships with other people.

Jesus summed up the primary importance of rightly living outwardly—with and toward other people—what we believe internally, this way: "Seek first the kingdom of God and his righteousness, and all these things [material needs] will be added to you."[10]

The Kingdom of God (the rule of his justice in the systems that give context and communal shape to people's lives) and his righteousness (right relationships among individuals and between those individuals and God) are to be the foundation for absolutely everything else in our lives. Finally, when we get to the Acts and the Epistles, we encounter a word that corresponds to our contemporary definition of religion.

The Greek word *thréskeia* (and its variants) doesn't have an inherently positive or negative connotation. It just means, essentially, the three core characteristics we identified in the introduction: (1) belief in a god or gods, (2) an organized system of beliefs (doctrines) about that or those gods, and (3) the activities, individual and communal, motivated by those beliefs. Any further meaning has to be derived from the context.

Paul used it to describe himself to King Agrippa as one who was an observant Jew: "They have known me for a long time and can testify, if they are willing, that I conformed to the strictest sect of our religion [*thréskeia*], living as a Pharisee."[11] It was part of his defense, so although the nature of his own religion had changed since meeting Jesus on the Damascus road, he meant it in an affirmative way.

In his letter to the Colossians, he encouraged the believers to dismiss the religious judgments others would try to lay on them. These people, he said, were falsely humble, and had "lost connection with the head"—their inner beliefs and outer actions were all askew and were not rooted in the character of Christ.[12] Bad religion, in other words. The kind of stuff that drives us crazy in contemporary Christendom.

And that brings us back to James, who described both bad religion and true religion in the same context. Here it is again, as a reminder:

> Those who consider themselves religious [*thréskeia*]
> and yet do not keep a tight rein on their tongues

deceive themselves, and their religion [*thréskeia*] is worthless. Religion that God our Father accepts as pure and faultless is this: to look after orphans and widows in their distress and to keep oneself from being polluted by the world.[13]

Our word *religion* is derived from the Latin word *religare*. This is the term used, in the passage above, in the Vulgate, the first translation of the New Testament from Greek to another language. Ancient Latin commentators said that it meant "to bind fast"—specifically, they said, to create "a bond between humans and gods,"[14] with the connection and obligation in both directions that such a bond implied. The Latin root, *ligare*, meaning "to bind," is where we get our English word *ligament*,[15] the name we give to the fibrous tissue that connects bone to bone in a human body and holds our organs in place.

It would be tempting to dismiss the implications of this Latin definition because it doesn't derive from the actual Greek word originally used by James. But there's a powerful image in the Old Testament that seems to correspond almost exactly to it, an image that could be very helpful to us in our struggle to claim a new, healthy, positive view of religious life.

THE VALLEY OF DRY BONES

The prophet Ezekiel had a vision:

> The hand of the LORD was on me, and he brought me out by the Spirit of the LORD and set me in the middle

> of a valley; it was full of bones. He led me back and
> forth among them, and I saw a great many bones on
> the floor of the valley, bones that were very dry. He
> asked me, "Son of man, can these bones live?"
> I said, "Sovereign LORD, you alone know."[16]

The scene makes me think of the "treasures" of the great cathedrals of Europe: dry bones. Long dead and powerless even though encased in gold and silver. And it makes me think, sadly, of the state of much organized religion today. There's lots of it—the bones carpet the entire floor of the valley—but it's still lifeless and dry. Can a church that seems increasingly irrelevant and out of step be brought back to vibrant life? God alone knows.

> He said to me, "Prophesy to these bones and say to
> them, 'Dry bones, hear the word of the LORD! This
> is what the Sovereign LORD says to these bones:
> I will make breath enter you, and you will come to
> life. I will attach tendons to you and make flesh come
> upon you and cover you with skin; I will put breath
> in you, and you will come to life. Then you will know
> that I am the LORD.'"[17]

Well, hooray! It *is* possible!

As the account continues, Ezekiel prophesies as God has commanded him. What happens next is like something out of a fantasy movie.

You have to picture it to get the power of the image: The

bones that fill the valley, long since bleached and dried out in the sun, begin to move, rattling and clicking against one another. They collide blindly, flipping and skittering and somehow shifting themselves until they begin to organize into coherent groups. They are not seeking the other bones that are like them—femurs and tibias and clavicles are not huddling in piles of their own kind. They are fitting themselves together, bone to bone in proper anatomical relationship, to create complete human skeletons.

The bones are all there, but there's nothing to bind them together. But wait: Tendons and ligaments and cartilage now are creeping like fast-growing vines between the bones, connecting them, drawing them tight. Knees, hips, elbows, and shoulders pop into place. Scattered vertebrae are bound into a sinuous line, connecting pelvis to rib cage to skull.

And then flesh begins to creep over the anonymous skeletons, granting them the form and identity of unique, individual people. Eyeballs appear, muscles and meat and skin and hair.

This is no longer a valley of dry bones. A dormant nation is stretched out here. As yet, there is no life in these bodies. Until . . .

He said to me, "Prophesy to the breath; prophesy, son of man, and say to it, 'This is what the Sovereign LORD says: Come, breath, from the four winds and breathe into these slain, that they may live.'" So I prophesied as he commanded me, and breath entered them; they came to life and stood up on their feet—a vast army.[18]

What an incredible vision of the quickening, the liveliness, that can come only from God! A vast army, ready to do battle with the forces of darkness, ready to wage war on hate, oppression, and poverty with the weapons of love, freedom, and generosity.

We see all around us the dry bones of dead or dysfunctional religion. At times, we may feel as though we're trapped somewhere in that valley ourselves. This is not what we want. We want that quickening. We want a cause so great it inspires us to live and die for it.

If faith is our skeleton, giving us form and a stable inner core, we want the strong ligaments of true religion to grant us movement. We want the flesh that is visible to the world to bear true witness to bones within. We want that body to be animated by the very breath of God.

True religion is to faith what a voice is to a thought. True religion is the articulated, inspirited movement of real faith.

True religion puts flesh on the bones of faith.

If *that's* religion, sign me up.

bad religion can feel so good

A WILD, PAGAN CHOIR keening in the night, distant but surely approaching by some erratic path. A blade of moonlight thrusting between invisible curtains severs the pitch of this room, one side cloven from the other without disturbing the essential darkness. A sword in its sheath. I rise from the bed and feel my way to the window, one bare questing foot seeking the way for the other.

I had not been sleeping anyway. Lying as usual with open eyes, staring upward into inky nothingness, mind and guts churning.

From this attic loft I can see clear across a lushly forested valley to the hills beyond. On their upper reaches they grow rugged, wearing here and there tatters of the blue mist that gives the Smokies their name; more of it floods the trough of the valley below. The moon has bleached the shivering leaves to bone. The cabin is perched on the mountainside, and the land abandons it without conscience. I feel as if, but for the log wall in which the window is set, it would pluck me off my feet and drag me down with it.

The moaning chorus as it approaches grows deeper, more diverse, more urgent. I wonder momentarily if I am dreaming this night, this place, these desolate voices, if they are only the ghosts of my own despair. The clamor rises to an apogee, and a split second before they burst into the cabin clearing, I know what it is: dogs.

The pack comes racing out of the woods, noses to the ground, tails in the air, all in a line like a necklace of beads being pulled in a hasty circle once around the cabin and off into the woods on the other side of the clearing. Coon hounds and beagles, I think, a dozen of them baying passionately after some unfortunate creature.

Their urgency touches me, the notes of longing and anguish in their voices, their frantic path through thick underbrush that must tear at their coats, the darkness. The determination to track down whatever they are hunting with only the smell of something ephemeral to draw them on.

But I am not here in an isolated log cabin on the side of a Carolina mountain because I am hunting. I am retreating. "A retreat"—that's what we call it. An escape. I am escaping, if only for a few days. I am here because if I didn't get away, put a long day of driving between myself and home, hunker down in a place where I am not known, something inside me would have snapped.

I grew up in that church. Almost all the people I love and admire most are there. I thought they knew me; I thought they trusted me. I thought the strength of our relationship would have borne easily the strain of my questions and growing conviction of a divergent view. I thought love was stronger than dogma, that at least if I was wrong, they would gently and patiently show me why. Instead I had been driven out.

I wish I could howl as the hounds do, howl and tear with such confidence into the night. As the pale trees and black pools of shadow swallow the last dog in line, I feel as if my soul is being driven into the darkness ahead of the pack. Looking for a crevice in the mountainside that might provide protection if I crawled in deep enough.

———————

James, the little brother of Jesus, struggled with the same thing we do. He was also surrounded by bad religion, crazy religion, vicious religion—and he was longing to live something real. The gods of the Romans justified their subjugation of most of the world the disciples of Jesus lived in—military incursion, economic oppression, and the implacable and bloody suppression of any revolt. Jewish people had experienced this before at the hands of Assyrians, Persians, and Greeks, among others. Furthermore, they had themselves, during the era of the Old Testament prophets, engaged in all manner of weird religious activities. They might have reached their all-time low during the time of the prophet Jeremiah when parents sacrificed their own children to the Ammonite god Molek.[1]

And James certainly saw bad religion much closer to home. The Pharisees were uptight, strictly religious folks who were only too ready to condemn anybody who didn't toe their very specific lines. The Sadducees were power-hungry politicians who used religious debate as a means of determining who was in or out and of justifying their own amoral political decisions. Does any of that sound familiar?

It certainly does to me. The folks I grew up among decried legalism and preached "grace alone" as the means of salvation. But at the same time, they often insisted on narrow and highly idiosyncratic interpretations of Scripture that seemed in direct contrast. We saw ourselves as guardians of the truth, as if God were unable to protect it on his own. In my early twenties, when I began to question some of our assumptions in pursuit of a greater understanding of that same truth, I was shocked to find that I had shifted quickly from "favored son" to "dangerous man."

I had reached a crisis point in my faith, and although I longed to live what I believed, my way of life had been so constrained by dogma and church culture that I could not imagine a way forward. The specific nature of the doctrinal wrangle that left me feeling betrayed and bereft hardly matters now—such disputes, and the vicious language and behaviors that accompany them, are as common as dirt within the church and just as filthy.

Several times I was tempted to swallow my questions and disquiet so that I'd simply be able to stay among the people

I loved. God kept calling me gently onward. It wasn't theoretical; this was real life. I headed to my friend's cabin in the hills of North Carolina in desperation, aware that what were then the most important relationships in my life were on the line.

Stepping out of the empty religion of his youth must have been even more fraught for James. This is how close to the bone it got for him—it was the most religious people of James's day who fabricated evidence, ran an illegal trial, and ultimately insisted on the murder of his brother Jesus.

A CHANGED MAN

Up to some point shortly after the Resurrection, it seems likely that James was probably a conservative-leaning, normally religious Jewish man. He doesn't seem to have thought very highly of the claims of Jesus: There's no mention of him by name, ever, among the followers of Jesus during his life. The Gospel of John states flat out that "even his own brothers did not believe in him."[2] Apart from attending the wedding in Cana—the one time James probably did show up, with his mothers and other brothers—Jesus wouldn't even leave the house where he was speaking to meet with them. Instead, he dismissed them with the comment, "My mother and brothers are those who hear God's word and put it into practice."[3]

Ouch. That had to hurt. Can you blame James, really, if he wasn't his big brother's biggest fan at first? Can you imagine growing up in the shadow of *Jesus*, of all people? Hearing all the older folks in town nattering on and on about what a sweet boy, what a wonderful youth, what a truly splendid young man Jesus was? It would be enough to make any younger brother sick. No, I wouldn't be at all surprised if he formed the same sort of opinion as those same townsfolk did later on, after Jesus came back from preaching around the countryside and, oh, raising the dead and things like that.

> "Where did this man get these things?" they asked.
> "What's this wisdom that has been given him? What
> are these remarkable miracles he is performing?
> Isn't this the carpenter? Isn't this Mary's son and the
> brother of James, Joseph, Judas and Simon? Aren't his
> sisters here with us?" *And they took offense at him.*[4]

Jesus, it seemed to them, had just gotten too big for his britches. It was so bad he was unable to do any miracles there, except the small stuff—laying his hands on a few sick people and healing them.[5]

But that all changed for James when the Pharisees and Sadducees ganged up on Pilate and manipulated him into crucifying Jesus. The risen Jesus seems to have appeared to more than five hundred other people first[6]—he certainly wasn't playing favorites with family members—but once he also had a little post-resurrection heart-to-heart with James, the deal was done. James's commitment to his old way of religious life was finished.

Now his challenge was to find a way to live out what he had come to believe. His old religion, despite a mother and father who had encountered angels and a cousin who was renowned as a prophet, hadn't had space in it for a messiah who happened to be his brother; it was, perhaps, as much a matter of habit and culture as of real faith. Every step of this new faith was a step into uncharted territory.

To his credit, James didn't just withdraw to a small town in Galilee and keep his head down. It would have been understandable, given that he would certainly have been on the watch list of the people who killed his brother. But what he had experienced was so powerful, so big, that he knew it couldn't remain only personal and private—it had to be shared, both in telling it and living it. This new faith had to be expressed publicly and communally.

It appears that James dove in headfirst. At some point, he seems to have become the acknowledged leader of the church in Jerusalem, perhaps after James, the brother of John, was beheaded.[7] He was certainly the one person Paul sought out when Paul returned to Jerusalem after his sojourn in the Arabian desert.[8] An early church letter ascribed to Clement of Rome calls him "the bishop of bishops, who rules Jerusalem."[9]

According to Josephus, the Jew who wrote history books for the Romans, James was executed in AD 62. Apparently, the local Jewish leaders appealed to him to tell those pesky Christians that following Jesus was a big mistake—it didn't conform to their religion. Hegesippus, another chronicler of the early church, quoted James's response: "[Christ] Himself sitteth in heaven, at the right hand of the Great Power, and shall come on the clouds of heaven."[10]

Whoops. And they thought James was tame.

After a hastily convened and, yes, illegal Sanhedrin condemned him, James was stoned to death. Déjà vu all over again. Josephus, who was no friend to Christians, commented that it was widely viewed as judicial murder.

You and I find bad religion frustrating, embarrassing, and even frightening. But it actually killed James.

And it's still happening, isn't it? As I write this, terrorist attacks have just a short time ago claimed the lives of a dozen people, this time in France.[11] A Muslim man, whose brother was shot and killed by other Muslims in the attacks, is being quoted in news accounts as saying, "My brother was Muslim and he was killed by people who pretend to be Muslims. They are terrorists, that's it."[12] For Islam as for Christianity, it's a relative handful of extremists who provide the popular caricature of the average adherent.

Christians killed other Christians during the Rwandan genocide of the 1990s. Muslims and Christians killed one another in Bosnia during roughly the same period, and Irish Catholics and Protestants finally ceased thirty years of mutual murder only in 1998. It's depressing, to say the least.

(Can we pause here to observe that, as a national ideology, atheism has done no better, and if anything, worse? Estimates of the murders at the hands of Joseph Stalin range from twenty to sixty million Soviet citizens. Pol Pot is thought to have slaughtered about a quarter of his eight million fellow Cambodians. During Mao Zedong's twenty-seven-year rule, about one million Chinese people *per year* died in prison and labor camps, and at least that many again from starvation. This doesn't appear to be the sort of "truth" that will set people free either. While religious maniacs are inclined to kill people who believe differently, atheist maniacs appear to have a genius for killing their own. Atheist apologists don't tend to dwell on this much.)

James, the conservative, don't-get-involved, resentful younger brother, decided to live above the deadly fumes of toxic religion. But he knew that the answer to bad religion wasn't an absence of religion. He couldn't just dismiss what he'd learned from and about Jesus. He couldn't just internalize it. He had to live it.

His short little letter isn't a treatise on a systematic theology. It's not even a thesis with a clearly articulated central statement and supporting arguments. It's not exactly an intimate communication to a close friend, either, addressed as it is "to the twelve tribes scattered among the nations." He doesn't describe himself as the brother of our Lord Jesus Christ or even as the bishop of Jerusalem—just, simply, as "a servant of God and of the Lord Jesus Christ."[13]

This is a letter containing the wisdom of one who has struggled to live out, in the real world and in real time, what Jesus taught. And it's written to others who are trying to do the same in the face of persecution, conflicted religious and social values, and the usual perplexing range of personal inclinations and quirks. Much like you and me (except, usually, for the persecution part). James doesn't write in an ordered fashion, clarifying each individual matter before marching on to the next one. As we do in conversation, he has something to say about a particular issue, which leads him to comment on something else, and then after a while he circles back to add another observation to the first matter, and so on.

I should note that, although we will assume that James

wrote this letter before there were any Gospels to read, we'll also make the reasonable assumption that he heard at least some of the teaching of Jesus verbatim, perhaps even before Jesus' public ministry began, as well as hearing lots later from the mouths of people who followed Jesus more closely than James had at the time. We'll try to read the letter as its first readers may have, picking up the handful of themes that emerge, themes that are clearly rooted in the teaching of Jesus.

(Can you imagine what it must have been like around the supper table at the Ben Joseph house when James was a kid? Jesus, functioning as the head of the household long after his father's death, passes the lentils and remarks casually, "You know, people who are poor in spirit really are blessed. In fact, the Kingdom of Heaven belongs to them!" James rolls his eyes and whispers to his younger brother Simon, "Here we go . . . again.")

These themes are all about putting flesh on the bones of faith, escaping the deadliness of religion that is merely rules and ritual. They're about not only believing in Jesus for ourselves but also living it together in a world that alternately bullies, seduces, and lulls us to sleep.

My short stay in that North Carolina cabin took place more than thirty years ago, but I still remember how confused and desperate I felt. For me, it turned out to be the beginning of a long catharsis. The incredible pressure I felt to conform, and the cold rejection I experienced when, in all conscience,

I couldn't, squeezed me like toothpaste from a tube, out of the restrictive container into a much wider world.

As exciting as that new world appeared, I grieved for much of what I had left behind. Those people were good people, loving and generous with their own. They knew what they believed, and they lived it, even when that meant rejecting someone they cared deeply about—a strange integrity. The sense of belonging had been so complete that I hadn't known it was there until it began to fray. I had, at one time, been trusted and well thought of; part of the reason it took so long to leave was that I didn't want these people whom I loved and respected to think ill of me. They had been my world, and I didn't yet know who I would be in this new one. Until I dared raise a challenge, I had been so very comfortable.

Bad religion can feel so good. Comforting forms and rituals, the sense of being an insider, clarity about who belongs to *us* and who belongs to *them*, the certainty that we are right and they are wrong, knowing exactly what behaviors are or are not approved, a manageable God who may require much of us but still stays within the carefully defined boundaries of our theological system. James did not find these things easy to give up, and neither did I.

The dogmas that shape our thinking as we grow up ultimately form a deeply ingrained default system of assumptions to which we instinctively return, especially when we are faced with situations or concepts we find difficult to understand. They become the unconscious foundation of the way we view the world, and we do not let go of them easily.

For James, it required the death and resurrection of his

brother Jesus to begin to pry the old, rote religion from his grasp. For me, it took this crisis, but for both of us, the struggle to live a new, true religion turned out to be a lifelong venture. At times it seems to me that my adult journey has featured an endless cycle of demolishing assumption after assumption about who God is and how he works in the world; I replace these assumptions with new, slightly roomier ones, which last for a time before being demolished themselves, and on I go. Often, these demolitions have been accompanied by feelings of anxiety and disorientation: *Who am I, and who, then, is God, if this foundation upon which I have built my understanding of both is flawed?*

Slowly, I am coming to realize how absurd it is for me to tell God who he is and how he should operate and expect him to stick to it. I had believed that defining God equaled knowing him; now I see that, as my certainties about him crumble, he grows bigger. Better. More gloriously loving and merciful and powerful.

CHAPTER FIVE

believe it or not

IT MUST HAVE BEEN ten years after listening to the eerie chant of the coon hounds on that moonlit night in North Carolina that I stood on a corner of Yonge Street in downtown Toronto and watched Billy get saved. Again.

It was late on one of those soft summer nights, when the warm, humid air seems to lie so tenderly on the skin. A strip of deep purple sky rippled the length of the street between the tips of the tall buildings looming above. Billy had been panhandling up and down a block or two of Yonge just south of Bloor, but despite the crowds on the sidewalks, he hadn't been doing much business. Billy was a little too random—he didn't have a line of patter or a gimmick; had never figured out how to look the punters manfully in the eye; tried to give a friendly grin, which looked more like a toothless leer; and was dressed in clothing that, while properly ragged, was frankly too dirty.

A church youth group had discovered him, though, and ensconced him at a café table with a large coffee and some sort of gooey muffin. I imagine they were cruising the downtown core in order to minister to the lost, and Billy certainly seemed to fit the description. The young people jammed themselves around him, one leaning on the back of another, their faces lit with excitement and pleasure. One intense teenager had seated himself opposite Billy; he had a large Bible open on the table and was reading from it, tracing the lines with his finger. He spun it around, finger still on the spot, so Billy could read it for himself. Billy was methodically two-fisting the coffee and the muffin.

He nodded slowly and peered at the finger on the Bible. After considering it carefully for thirty seconds or so—the finger or the passage, I wasn't sure which—he looked up and mumbled a question. The teenager hitched his chair still closer and began to explain something earnestly. I smiled. Billy had set the hook.

I had seen this before, but I have to admit I admired his artistry as he reeled the entire youth group in. He was in no rush. He had some coffee and a mouthful of the muffin left, and the attention of seven or eight beautiful young people—a rare occurrence, indeed, in Billy's world. They talked on, Billy and the intense teenage evangelist. Billy made slow, crumb-strewn queries after long, pondering silences; the evangelist pounced on his questions with eager, definitive answers. The circle around them tightened, leaned farther in.

Finally, Billy nodded; the group sighed as one and loosened their cordon. The young evangelist reached out a hand, placing it on Billy's shoulder, and Billy bowed his head.

I knew it wasn't over yet. As Billy looked up, beaming, the young evangelist shook his hand and a few members of the group patted his shoulders. Billy was speaking now, with a degree of focus and range of expression that hadn't been evident earlier. He stood, smiling broadly, and, turning from one kid to the next, patted *their* shoulders as he explained something to them. The young people looked suddenly wary.

Sensing it, Billy turned back to the teenage evangelist, who was still simpering horribly, and made a plea every bit as impassioned as the one he'd been listening to a few minutes earlier. This time, it was the evangelist who listened long, and he slowly nodded. He reached into his back pocket and then withdrew his wallet.

One by one, each member of the youth group did the same. Even from where I was standing, their inner conflict was easily read in their body language and on their faces. But all of them gave Billy something, and a few bold souls even gave him awkward hugs. On the whole, they looked quite pleased and excited as they marched away, waving back at Billy and calling out blessings to him as they went. And Billy—well, Billy was radiant.

I think all involved went home happy that night.

LISTEN, LOOK, AND LIVE

I wonder how often James thought about that time he tried to visit Jesus with his mother and brothers while Jesus was preaching. I imagine that he went along mostly to please Mary, but perhaps he also thought, *Well, Jesus may be a little left of center, but he's still my brother. I should probably show up for form's sake, if nothing else.* He likely thought Jesus would at least ask the crowd to make way so his mom and brothers would be able to be with him in the middle of it all. He might even have hoped that Jesus would make a bit of a fuss over them, introduce them to the crowd or something. But no—"My mother and brothers are those who hear God's word and put it into practice."[1]

As aggravating as it must have been to hear that at the time, the converted James later recognized the simple, fundamental truth in Jesus' words.

> Do not merely listen to the word, and so deceive yourselves. Do what it says. Anyone who listens to the word but does not do what it says is like someone who looks at his face in a mirror and, after looking at himself, goes away and immediately forgets what he looks like. But whoever looks intently into the perfect law that gives freedom, and continues in it—not forgetting what they have heard, but doing it—they will be blessed in what they do.[2]

Listening but not doing equals self-deception. I would bet that this is the most common criticism of Christians by others: We don't actually do the things Jesus did or said we should. We listen endlessly to preaching, music, podcasts, radio programs, and more that are supposed to spur us to action, but we live pretty much the same way everybody else does. We're attending church (or not) instead of being the church.

Jesus quoted Isaiah to describe the Pharisees, those

clean-living, morally upright, by-the-book, synagogue-going, patriotic, finger-pointing, Bible-studying, punctiliously rule-following, compassion-challenged, cream-of-the-crop exemplars of conservative Hebrew faith: "These people honor me with their lips, but their hearts are far from me. They worship me in vain; their teachings are merely human rules."[3]

They had looked in the mirror, walked away, and promptly forgotten who they were supposed to be. Doesn't it send a chill through you? Nobody reads the Gospels and wants to be like the Pharisees. So how come we often look very much like them?

The mirror into which we are supposed to look *intently* (the same word Luke and John use to describe Peter stooping down to gaze into the empty tomb of Christ) is something James calls "the perfect law that gives freedom." Just looking into it, and continuing to do so while acting out the word we have listened to, will ensure that we remember who we are and that our "doing" will be blessed.

But what is this law? He mentions it again in the next chapter:

> Speak and act as those who are going to be judged by the law that gives freedom, because judgment without mercy will be shown to anyone who has not been merciful. Mercy triumphs over judgment.[4]

How different from our laws, which create restrictions and punish the offender! Whatever *this* law is, it values mercy—clemency for the offender—over being sure that we have it all right. And the purpose of this law is to give freedom, so it's certainly not about being bound by all the rules. Simply believing it in our hearts won't do; we must speak and act according to its dictates. The clear implication here is that this law doesn't just guide our speech and activities; it compels them.

Some say that the law is mercy itself; others say that the law is gospel or even freedom. I think that mercy is the character of "the perfect law," freedom is its result, and the gospel is its context. *Perfect* here means "fully developed, complete." It's not a specific codicil among God's communications to humanity. It's the big picture, the summation of all that the Mosaic law, plus the teaching of Christ, was intended to guide us to. Jesus himself summed it up in two positive, proactive phrases: (1) Love God; love your neighbor. (2) Do this and you'll live.[5] Later, alone with his closest disciples, Jesus puts a still finer point on it, delivering his new commandment or law: "Love one another" / "Love each other."[6]

"If the Son sets you free, you will be free indeed,"[7] Jesus said to his disciples. I think Jesus himself is the expression of this perfect law, the summation of God's word to humanity. He is love; he is freedom. His person, his work, his teaching. Life, death, resurrection, and rule. In fact, the *word* that James tells us to listen to is, in the Greek text, *logou*, a derivative of *logos*, the term John uses to name Jesus "the Word" at the beginning of his Gospel.

So, then. Listen to Jesus. Look intently at Jesus. Live Jesus—do what Jesus does. Jesus—that's who we're supposed to see in the mirror. That's the image at which we are to gaze and into which we are to be slowly transformed.

Imagine if the church in this world, and the individuals

who make it up, actually looked and acted like Jesus. Instead of spending most of our time and resources on a razzle-dazzle Sunday morning service, together we'd heal the sick, feed the hungry, embrace the unwelcome, set prisoners free, restore the dignity of people who have been humiliated, flip the tables of oppressive economics, offer forgiveness instead of seeking vengeance, sacrifice rather than protect ourselves, and much, much more. We'd vote for governments that promised to do those things, instead of caving to the miserable, miserly, faith-starved inducement of tax reduction or other me-first policies. White police officers and young black men would embrace and pray together. We'd send armies of servants instead of soldiers to less fortunate countries; we would overwhelm our enemies with love and self-sacrifice. We'd be content with having enough, and rather than continually seeking more, more, more, we'd share our excess with those who don't have enough. We'd do all this as well as announcing the Good News of salvation for the individual soul—in fact, we'd do all this as a means of announcing it. Because that's what Jesus did.

Even the neediest of my friends at Sanctuary—men and women who struggle with addiction, mental illness, post-traumatic disorders, and extreme poverty—know that this is what Jesus followers are supposed to look like.

Every now and then, when I can't, or for some good reason won't, supply one of my friends with something he or she wants—a sleeping bag, a meal, the freedom to continue abus ing someone else in the community—that person will shout at me, "You call yourself a Christian? Jesus wouldn't do this! I'm homeless! You *have* to [insert expectation here]!"

Of course, I've cleaned their words up a lot—my friends employ the vernacular with extravagance and verve, even if it generally lacks a little creative scope. Still, as silly and unreasonable as it most often is in the moment, my heart always twists a little when I hear that. Because, really, that person may not understand him- or herself very well, but their understanding of Jesus is pretty good. And I'm not a very good likeness. Like the birds and foxes, I have a place to lay my head at night. I'm not poor or persecuted. So in these regards, my homeless friends look more like Jesus than I do. Sometimes I decline to act just because I'm tired or hungry myself.

So it's daunting, this look-like-Jesus thing. It's great to think about the whole church doing and being that, but it's overwhelming to consider it on a personal level. Jesus himself didn't sugarcoat it when he told his disciples,

> Whoever wants to be my disciple must deny
> themselves and take up their cross daily and follow
> me. For whoever wants to save their life will lose it,
> but whoever loses their life for me will save it.[8]

Hmm. That's not the upbeat, comforting message we tend to hear on Sundays, is it? Pick up my cross? Lose my life in order to save it? Not much of a salesman, Jesus. And it doesn't get any easier:

> What good is it for someone to gain the whole world,
> and yet lose or forfeit their very self? Whoever is

ashamed of me and my words, the Son of Man will be
ashamed of them when he comes in his glory.[9]

James, it seems to me, had actually experienced this. He
had lost his former self, given up that life. He could no longer
expect to plod along in the comfortable obscurity of a small
town, running the family construction business and trying to
keep up with the Ben Joneses. His brother's death was a kind
of death for him, too; he had picked up his own cross and was
now following in Jesus' turbulent wake. But he had been delivered—resurrected, you could almost say—to a new and larger
life, one in which the former values and restrictions no longer
applied. But living bigger didn't mean that he didn't still have
his feet on the ground.

James witnessed it: The life and teaching of Jesus wasn't
just high-flying spiritual rhetoric, a kind of detachment that
leaves one untouched by the needs of others. Forgiving sins
went hand in hand with healing the infirm—and the more
mundane matter of feeding people who were hungry. The message was never only about saving souls, and saving souls was
never a matter of touch-and-go conversion.

After this fairly exalted talk of gazing into the law that gives
freedom, and speaking and acting according to what we see
and the mercy we find there, James gives us a very practical,
down-to-earth example of what it looks like when we don't.

What good is it, my brothers and sisters, if someone
claims to have faith but has no deeds? Can such faith
save them? Suppose a brother or a sister is without

clothes and daily food. If one of you says to them, "Go in peace; keep warm and well fed," but does nothing about their physical needs, what good is it? In the same way, faith by itself, if it is not accompanied by action, is dead.[10]

What good is it if you just want to get stuff and keep it for yourself? Jesus says. *What good is it* if you don't share what you have with someone in need? James asks.

What good is your faith, then? It doesn't matter how deep, intensely personal, and private your spirituality is. It will cost you your very self if it doesn't give issue to material expression. You'll begin to believe something other than the truth about who you are in Christ. We have to pick up and carry our respective crosses, just like Jesus did. Our faith has to do good in order to be good. Faith that doesn't compel us to act in practical ways that supply the needs of people around us is dead, done, useless, moldering in the grave, rotting and stinking to—literally!—high heaven.

It's striking that James refers here to people who are without "daily food." These aren't folks who are without food because they forgot to pack a lunch. Their lives are in a settled condition of continual hunger. Getting involved with them will not just mean handing off a sandwich, as some well-meaning church outreach groups do from time to time in the downtown core of my city. Nor will it be restricted to a concern for their spiritual welfare only. It will mean *doing something about their physical needs*. Regarding the one who blesses and "does nothing about their physical needs, what good is it?" James asks. Doing something. Living it. Finding a way to change the conditions that keep that brother or sister hungry and underclothed, while keeping him or her warm and fed in the interim.

By the way, let's not fool ourselves that "a brother or a sister" means we can keep our giving and game-changing activities within the "family of faith." Even gangsters look after their own people. When Jesus said, "Whatever you did for one of the least of these brothers and sisters of mine,"[11] he made it abundantly clear that all hungry, thirsty, foreign, naked, sick, or imprisoned people are his siblings and ours.

This isn't a church summer or Christmas program, is it? There will always be people who are hungry and need clothing. A 2010 study published by the National Center for Children in Poverty (NCCP) said that fourteen million children in the States are growing up in poverty—19 percent of American children, and the percentage has been climbing for years. Almost half the nation's children live in low-income families, where food security may be an issue.[12] Analysts of Statistics Canada data deduce that about 1.3 million kids are growing up in poor families, about 19 percent of children in Canada.[13]

Christian countries? I don't think so. Both Canada and the States rank in the bottom third of all "developed" countries for indicators of child poverty.

So no, the church youth group slinging soup down at the mission on an annual basis or doing evangelistic theater on the street isn't what James is talking about. He's not talking about programs; he's talking about a way of life. If the struggling people he describes have a daily need of food, then you and I have a daily need of involvement with them. That's true religion. Faith with some meat on its bony frame.

Believing in Jesus for my own salvation and stopping there is a profoundly ungrateful way to live, given what it cost God—and it's hardly a life of faith at all.

"Show me your faith without deeds," James says, "and I will show you my faith by my deeds. You believe that there is one God. Good! Even the demons believe that—and shudder."[14]

Yikes. Just believing in God isn't very impressive, then, not if even the demons believe. Perhaps we should shudder too, because, like them, what we believe about God so often doesn't line up with the way we act. James rams the point home a little later: "If anyone, then, knows the good they ought to do and doesn't do it, it is sin for them."[15]

I wonder, when I read this, if James had heard the simple little parable Jesus had tossed at those good religious folk, the Pharisees: A man with two sons asked both of them to do some work in the family vineyard. One refused, but later changed his mind and went off and did the work. The second politely agreed—"I will, sir"—but goofed off. The yes-sir-no-sir-whatever-you-say-sir Pharisees, who would then promptly about-face and pursue their own comfortable agenda rather than God's, would, Jesus proclaimed, be beaten into the Kingdom of God by tax collectors and prostitutes.[16]

The bottom line here is this: If you say you believe it—but you don't do it—you don't believe it.

If we choose lower taxes or tithes over food for the hungry and healing for the sick, or think paying attention to the worship band is more important than paying attention to the single mom slugging it out as a Walmart cashier, or believe the cause of freedom means the people of our nation are more valuable to God than those of another country, or pray for people in need but don't share what we have with them . . . well, then, we just don't believe what Jesus taught.

We need to go work in the vineyard.

But listen, there's good news: We do not work for our salvation; we work because salvation is already at work in us.

OPEN YOUR HANDS

At the time that I witnessed Billy's masterful handling of that youth group, I had already been involved in some form of outreach on the streets of Toronto for almost twenty years. The traumatic exit from the church of my youth was years in the past, although it would not be accurate to say that I was then completely over it. Despite such lengthy previous experience of hanging out on the street with hustlers of one sort or another, or in bars with the kind of folks for whom the local pub is a combination of home and church, I, too, had arrived quite convinced that I had meaningful answers for people who often weren't even sure what the questions were.

My earlier experience had involved touch and go activities—doing outreach for an evening or playing a gig in a bar,[17] then going back home to "real" life. It took only a short while of walking day by day, every day, beside some of the poorest and most excluded people in the city—men and women whose lives had been smashed by repeated traumas, psychiatric illness, and the homelessness and addictions that often resulted—to discover that my "answers" were irrelevant, my solutions ineffective. I had been trained to deliver the gospel in much the same manner as those young evangelists, but the needs of those excluded people would not submit to the solutions my doctrinal convictions prescribed. Life would not conform to theory.

The enthusiasm of that youth group for sharing with Billy about the forgiveness and salvation available to him through the Cross was really quite lovely. But they had no idea at all who Billy really was, what his life was like, or what he understood his real, immediate needs to be. He managed to wangle some cash out of them—his goal from the moment the conversation first began—but they had essentially said to one who had need of clothes and daily food, "Go in peace; keep warm and well fed."[18] I don't doubt the sincerity of those young people. Unfortunately, the narrowness of the gospel they had been taught, their naivete, and Billy's material needs and street smarts combined to make a mockery of the salvation they offered him.

Now, I had at least come to understand that following Jesus and announcing Good News in the real, workaday world meant going where he went and doing what he did. I was beginning to understand that even this wasn't just about what I believed and how I lived it out personally; true religion meant living it out together, day by day, with others.

Living life with Billy day by day looked very different from "converting" him over coffee and muffins. And there were hundreds of Billys in our neighborhood; trying to meet the needs of even one was more than I could manage. It was unnerving to have the pillars of my certainties knocked out from under me. It was humbling to discover that my efforts were often ineffective. But what at times felt like snowballing catastrophe turned out to be a series of gifts.

I discovered that I needed my friends as much as they needed me, and that this mutual need was the linchpin of Kingdom community. There were innumerable little ways, I saw, in which they were blessed already, just as Jesus said they were—and some of this blessing began to rub off on me. Dimly, I began to realize that God was far, far bigger than I had ever imagined or could imagine, and so was his gospel; that my own competence and convictions, while still of some value, were not even close to being the point; *that it wasn't up to me to rescue or convert anyone*. That was God's job. What a relief.

It *was* up to me to walk with them. I began to revel in the joy of loving and being loved—loved!—by dozens of people who had nothing else to give. And by giving their love to me, they taught me this: God is not in the business of giving answers; he is in the business of giving himself.

To receive a gift, you have to open your hands. I had wrapped my fists tightly around my own dogmas and putative abilities; only by releasing my hold on them could I begin to accept what God offered. To see clearly, you have to look past the familiar—you have to open your eyes and really look. I had to release my previous view of both God and people to see something I hadn't recognized before: God is among us, with us, for us, just as surely as Jesus was so long ago, and often in the most surprising form.

I have sat beside Jesus in a dying man, held him in the shape of a homeless young girl, smelled him in the soiled clothing of one lost in addiction, tasted him in shared bread and wine, and heard his voice in the cry of one tortured by loss and even mental illness. I have found him—or he has found me—in such circumstances in a manner deeper and more tangible by far than in any expression of a safe, sanitized religion.

Mightier and humbler, purer and more gritty, wilder and more tender, holier and more broken than ever I could have imagined. That's gospel.

CHAPTER SIX

living the beatitudes

MATT WAS A SLENDER, dark-haired man who always seemed younger than his age. He invariably dressed well and possessed a substantial amount of the kind of charm that engages some and irritates others. I suppose it was the appearance of a normal capacity to be responsible and respectful to others, and his frequent contrary actions, that put me off him. I should have known better.

He lived for a while with the family of Doug Johnson Hatlem, who was, at the time, a member of the Sanctuary staff. Jodi, Doug's wife, told me later about how really great Matt was with the kids—attentive, tender, funny, and completely trustworthy. He eagerly helped out in the house wherever he could. His addiction issues eventually meant he couldn't keep living with them, but I don't think the Johnson Hatlems ever stopped viewing Matt as a member of the family.

He had usually seemed to me to be cheerfully oblivious to the harm he caused. At other times, he would be appalled, profusely apologetic, and bitterly self-condemning, hardly able to believe what he had done—but completely unable to keep from doing it again.

Matt's death, especially the nature of it, took everyone by surprise. Earlier on the day he died, he had called Steve, the only man who ever really acted as a father toward him, and said that he was on his way from one northern Ontario city to another in order to get into rehab. Instead, he stopped along the highway, trudged to a nearby barn, and took his own life. He was in his early thirties.

BUILDING ON THE BEATITUDES

When James writes, "Religion that God our Father accepts as pure and faultless is this," he's saying that what's to follow is the nut of how we are to live out, publicly and communally, what we believe about God privately and individually. Given his personal frame of reference, I think it would be reasonable to say that, if James were pressed to boil down everything about living Jesus' teachings to one distilled droplet, it would be this. Here's the whole critical statement:

> Religion that God our Father accepts as pure and faultless is this: to look after orphans and widows in their distress and to keep oneself from being polluted by the world.[1]

We need to unpack this a bit because James is giving us a concise description of what true religion does. It's his way, I think, of summarizing what we're supposed to actually do with Jesus' teaching, specifically the Beatitudes. In fact, he explicitly references them just a bit further on in his description of pure, faultless religion:

> Listen, my dear brothers and sisters: Has not God chosen those who are poor in the eyes of the world to be rich in faith and to inherit the kingdom he promised those who love him?[2]

As we'll see, James references the ideas in the Beatitudes repeatedly, so let's back up a bit here and give some thought to the body of teaching that James is wrestling with. It should go without saying that this should be important to us anyway, as people who want to really follow Jesus as Master and not just grab our salvation and run.

Most Bible scholars agree that the Sermon on the Mount is the centerpiece of Jesus' teaching. Even people who don't like God or Jesus much can read it and agree that it is brilliant stuff, the kind of teaching about life and how to live it that is just so common-sense in parts and so radical in others—the kind of direction, in short, that everybody should follow and most of us don't.

The Sermon on the Mount—and to a slightly lesser extent, the Sermon on the Plain related by Luke—present what might be called the Charter of the Kingdom of God or the Declaration of Independence from the Rule of Small, Insular

Living. And the Beatitudes, right at the very beginning of the Sermon, are the beautiful, powerful, culturally subversive preamble that sets both tone and context for the rest. They are a description of the salvation that's at work in us, the salvation that compels us—to the degree that we also believe what Jesus taught by word and deed before being crucified—to work. Actually doing this work—going to the vineyard when he asks us to—is how we make him Lord in our lives.

In case it's been a while since you read them, here are those Beatitudes:

Blessed are the poor in spirit,
    for theirs is the kingdom of heaven.
Blessed are those who mourn,
    for they will be comforted.
Blessed are the meek,
    for they will inherit the earth.
Blessed are those who hunger and thirst for
      righteousness,
    for they will be filled.
Blessed are the merciful,
    for they will be shown mercy.
Blessed are the pure in heart,
    for they will see God.
Blessed are the peacemakers,
    for they will be called children of God.
Blessed are those who are persecuted because of
      righteousness,
    for theirs is the kingdom of heaven.[3]

The blessedness that Jesus pronounces over and over is "a quality of spirituality that is already present";[4] the people he describes are, as far as he's concerned, favored by God here and now. These lucky folks are at the core of God's plans for his people and his creations. It's the rest of the description of them that proves surprising.

At first glance, it looks as though Jesus might have gotten the order mixed up. Shouldn't people who are so bold in living righteously (living the justice of God's Kingdom in relationship with others), so determined to live according to God's direction that they experience persecution, be right at the top of the list? Working in reverse order, we could understand it if, at the end of the day, there's even room in the Kingdom of Heaven for people who are, well, spiritually poor.

But Hebrew literary sensibility always puts the most important stuff at the beginning. Jesus clearly meant what he said and meant to say it exactly the way he did. "Blessed are the poor in spirit, for theirs is the kingdom of heaven." Starting here flips society's norms and expectations upside down. It shouldn't be such a surprise, really. Didn't Jesus warn us that "the last will be first, and the first will be last"?[5]

Still, this is such a radical, countercultural foundation for gospel living, and always has been, that followers of Jesus have done theological and interpretive gymnastics generation after generation to avoid the inconvenience of trying to really embrace it.

Theological systems have been developed that teach that all of Jesus' teaching about the Kingdom of Heaven is really only for that unknown time in the future when Christ will return and the Kingdom will be finally and fully established.[6] Such systems have effectively gutted the Gospels and rendered Jesus irrelevant to our daily lives except as a sacrifice for sin. It's as if the teachings of our Master were gathered and placed in a time capsule, to be opened only at the end of time.

Really? Jesus stood there among the crowds of people who were diseased, in severe pain, demon possessed, and afflicted with seizures and paralysis[7] and told them a bunch of stuff that wouldn't apply for at least two thousand years? And he's *still* talking past you and me today?

The other approach that has robbed the Beatitudes and much of the rest of Jesus' teaching of its power has been to spiritualize it until it is a kind of pabulum that anyone could swallow. In this idiom, "the poor in spirit" are those who recognize and admit their spiritual poverty—essentially, if we are humble, we'll be blessed. Well, okay. That's not so hard.

But it isn't at all what Jesus meant.

These Beatitudes aren't aspirational. We aren't supposed to want to be like that so we can get the blessing—cash in on the Kingdom, be comforted, inherit the earth, and so on. The blessedness Jesus describes already exists in these folks. Jesus is telling us who the Kingdom is for, who is already at the center of it and of his blessing. He's not telling us this so that we can become poor in spirit, but so we'll know that people we might normally write off are at the heart of it all, so that we'll know we're welcome if we find ourselves among them, and especially so that we can orient ourselves to God's agenda.

The word *poor* here means, literally, "one who crouches and cowers like a beggar";[8] figuratively it indicates somebody

who is utterly destitute and lacking in any resource what-
soever. This isn't somebody who is humble; it's somebody
whose spirit has been pummeled until there's nothing left.
Jesus is talking about people who are spiritually battered and
bankrupted.

Some of my street-involved friends endured horrific abuse
as children, and consequently, live as adults with addictions,
post-traumatic issues, homelessness, self-abuse, and more.
Understandably, not a few of those believe that if there is a
God, he must hate them, and they hate him back. They're poor
in spirit. They're also blessed by God, because his Kingdom
is for them.

"Those who mourn," similarly, aren't just people who are
sad. These are people who are prostrated by grief, knocked
down, unable to cope or hide their lament.

I used to keep a list of people from our community who had
died, usually as a result of addictions, suicide, homelessness,
or murder. I stopped keeping the list many years ago, because
I could no longer bear to add another name to the dozens that
were already there. One friend lost four siblings and his mother
in the space of two years. Just yesterday, as I write, I received
word that another of his friends, Ramsey (my brother too!), was
murdered. We are never finished grieving one death before
another comes along.

In God's Kingdom, my friend is blessed because he will
be comforted. There's something interesting about the Greek
word for *comforted* that doesn't appear in the English. The
root word, sure enough, means to be comforted or consoled
as we would normally understand it. But there's a prefix

that indicates the comfort comes from someone who is close beside. This mourning becomes that which connects the mourner directly and intimately to God, and to others who will grieve with him or her.

Do you know anybody who wants to be known as *meek*? Me neither. But Jesus did: "Take my yoke upon you [work with me!] and learn from me, for I am gentle [or *meek*; a variant of the same word we've been looking at] and humble in heart, and you will find rest for your souls."[9] So Jesus was good with being meek, but look at how it worked out for him: abandoned, beaten, crucified.

That's what usually happens to meek people, isn't it? They get ignored, shoved around, banished to the outer perimeter of whatever group they're in. There are people like this in my community, too—women who get abused and handed around like secondhand paperbacks, men too physically weak or mentally ill to stand up for themselves. Native people who got shoved off their land generations ago and are still sequestered in the regions no one else wants. Poor people in general in our Western world, who get blamed for being poor in the first place and blamed again for being a drag on the economy, whom nobody listens to, who are so convinced of their own valuelessness that it seems pointless to vote, whose chances of ever escaping are so slim that crime can seem like the only viable option—who actually embrace the pernicious lie of their faultiness as the truth and then fulfill its awful insidious rottenness in their lives.

In the Kingdom of Heaven, these meek ones are blessed. The ones who have been driven to the margins and then ignored will inherit the earth—they'll get to go everywhere and anywhere, and everywhere they go they'll be at home. They're at the center of the Kingdom agenda.

You get the picture. Our purpose here is not a thorough exegesis of Jesus' teachings about his Kingdom, or even of the Beatitudes. We're just trying to get the flavor of citizenship in that Kingdom so that we can get an inkling of what it might mean to begin living it out. (See the appendix for an "expanded version" of the Beatitudes.)

LOOKING AFTER ORPHANS AND WIDOWS

All right, then. Jesus has made it clear where the focal point of Kingdom work is. Just like an earthquake, the shock waves of Kingdom influence and activity radiate from this surprising epicenter of the people who are rejected everywhere else, upsetting the structures and values of the world as we know it. This is what James was wrestling with. How, then, *do* we live it?

What, exactly, does he mean by "pure and faultless"? *Pure* is often translated as "clean" or "clear." The idea here is that the religion he's describing is the real thing, not watered down with or tainted by being mixed with something else; something transparent, not hiding more serious pollution within a general murk. *Faultless* would be better translated as "undefiled"—untainted, unstained, hasn't been contaminated. So both these words have a similar meaning, which is James's way of emphasizing that this is the gold standard of faith in action, all 24 karats of it.

There are two aspects to James's neat synopsis of what working faith looks like: (1) looking after widows and orphans and (2) keeping oneself from being polluted by the world. The latter is a substantial theme on its own, and we'll look more carefully at it in the next chapter. For now, let's focus on that first one.

To Look After Widows and Orphans in Their Distress

In referencing orphans and widows, James chooses the contemporary stereotype of the poorest, neediest, most vulnerable people in society. In a time when there was no social safety net at all and women couldn't legally inherit or own property, a woman whose husband died was left at the mercy of family members, if there were any. This, largely, is why the tradition developed of the brother of the deceased man taking his brother's widow as his own wife—but then, of course, the woman had ceased to be a widow and was a wife again. A widow was someone who had no one to protect or care for her, no equity and not much value to society. An orphan was even more so, and there were apparently lots of them, much as there are today in third world countries—little kiddies scrambling to survive in a society that has too little resources to go around, where even children with parents barely get enough to eat. Small and weak, easily denied or robbed of what they need to thrive. We've all seen them on late-night TV pitches from international relief organizations.

This is such a minimal issue for our "developed world" societies today that if you google "orphans and widows," you'll find a page full of references to typesetting terminology.

But James, the good Jewish boy, remembers the law of Moses, wherein Yahweh threatens reprisal to anyone who mistreats these vulnerable ones, making the oppressors' children and wives into orphans and widows too—pretty much the worst fate anyone could imagine for their families:

> You shall not mistreat any widow or fatherless child.
> If you do mistreat them, and they cry out to me, I will
> surely hear their cry, and *my wrath will burn, and I will
> kill you with the sword, and your wives shall become
> widows and your children fatherless.*[10]

I think James chooses orphans and widows as icons of all who are poor in spirit, mourning, meek, starving for justice. These are the Beatitudes for people who are at the very center of the Kingdom of Heaven. Today we might choose a homeless schizophrenic woman or a street kid who has been trafficked into sex work as a similar societal icon of extreme neediness in our own communities. These are people who are in *distress*—a term that describes being in a bad situation with no way out.

And how are we to *look after* them? This is a nuanced word (just one word in the Greek), with a few layers of meaning. The first of these is to actually *look upon* the person, really look, to examine him or her with your eyes. Not a casual glance, then.

On a recent visit to Manhattan, my wife, Maggie and I came across a man who clearly had psychiatric issues, hanging out near the foot of the Brooklyn Bridge. He was talking loudly to someone who wasn't there, gesticulating wildly, and walking energetically around in circles. His hands and clothes were grimy. I noticed how people looked away from the man—one quick glance, and then heads turned and eyes were fixed elsewhere as they gave the man a wide berth. Some even turned and walked back the way they had come. Normal reactions.

I also registered, perhaps because I was in another city and out of my usual context, my own reaction. Because over many recent years I have had the great joy and privilege of sharing life with a number of men and women who are street involved and struggling with psychiatric illness, my first thought wasn't *Whoa! Crazy guy. May be dangerous. Don't make eye contact! Get out of his path!* Instead, it was *Well, hello, brother!* There was an instinctive spark of recognition, a sense of connection, precisely because of the man's evident disorder.

We didn't interrupt the man's conversation, but we did stroll right through the circular path he was hustling around. He made way for us. What a gift to feel safe where others perceived only danger!

Those of us who are privileged to have more than enough must first look at the "orphans and widows" around us long enough to understand who they are and what the nature of their need is. In fact, we may even need to search them out, as poverty and vulnerability are such sources of shame in our society that people will go to great lengths to hide them. Who are the widows and orphans in your neighborhood?

Having looked on the orphans and widows in this way, James calls us to "look after" them—to make it our business to find out what they need and find a way to supply it. This certainly goes beyond material needs, although it just as certainly includes those. What do orphans and widows need most? To be brought into the family. It's no coincidence that James reminds us that this true religion is what is acceptable to God *the Father*. James remembers the numerous places in the Old Testament where Yahweh promises to be a father to the fatherless, to take widows under his wing. In some translations, this word is rendered "visit": the idea not of dropping by for a coffee and some scones, but of hanging out with and abiding with these people who have no one else to care for them. It means finding a way to live our lives together.

Once we've looked after our new family members for a while, we'll find we also want to *look out* for them. We'll want to equip them for the journey ahead, advocate for them with others, get them set up so that, eventually, they can not only care well for themselves but also begin caring for others.

That sounds like a whole-life journey with these orphans and widows, doesn't it? And it is. But it's not a journey to be undertaken alone. James calls this *religion*, and that reminds us that we, members of the body of Christ, are bones ligamented together, enfleshed with sinew, muscle, and skin; and our lungs are filled with the very breath of God for this purpose. Our individual, private faith compels us to do this work publicly and together.

To Keep Oneself from Being Polluted by the World

It's an evocative image, isn't it? We all know what pollution looks like: the brownish fog that hangs over most large cities in hot weather; dead fish among the cigarette packs and soft-drink bottles bobbing against harbor walls; smashed beer bottles left by some troglodyte at a wilderness campsite;

a dying duck smothered in oil. There's so much of it that it's changing our climate, slowly throttling the planet.

In spiritual terms, *pollution* has historically been of great concern to just about every religion. In the church culture I grew up in, watching TV was frowned upon, and movies and dancing were out of the question. In Old Testament times, the Israelites weren't supposed to have any truck with foreign gods or foreign women. Touching a dead animal in the field—a sometimes necessary act if you were the herdsman—made you unclean and necessitated offering a sacrifice. So did something as unavoidable as a woman's menstruation.

It was concern for this kind of ceremonial cleanness that kept the hypocrites who were railroading Jesus to his crucifixion from entering Pilate's headquarters: to do so would have defiled them and disqualified them from celebrating Passover.[11] Kill a man but don't get your hands dirty: precisely the approach that has given religion such an awful stink in our world. Don't say, "That's not really religion." It is. Those men were living out what they really believed: dotting the i's and crossing the t's of the religious rules was more important to them than actually doing the right thing. It's religion, all right—bad, toxic, evil religion.

Although the Levitical stipulations that led to such travesty don't affect us much today, some churches do reflect, perhaps unintentionally, this need for "ceremonial" purity by the practice of liturgical confessions before the Eucharist. Communal and individual confession are certainly good practice, but the impression I suspect many congregants are left with is "Now we are cleaning up ourselves enough to qualify for participation." A kind of spiritual quick scrub of the neck and behind the ears.

Examples abound of people, even and especially clergy, who scrupulously observe all the public religious forms while engaging in the most despicable behavior in their private lives, just like those murderous scribes and Pharisees.

But James is not referring to either moral or ceremonial pollution here. Removing the artificial chapter division, which only appeared for the first time in the Wycliffe Bible of 1382, makes James's intent immediately apparent. Here is how he describes being polluted by the world:

My brothers and sisters, believers in our glorious
Lord Jesus Christ must not show favoritism. Suppose
a man comes into your meeting wearing a gold ring
and fine clothes, and a poor man in filthy old clothes
also comes in. If you show special attention to the
man wearing fine clothes and say, "Here's a good
seat for you," but say to the poor man, "You stand
there" or "Sit on the floor by my feet," have you not
discriminated among yourselves and become judges
with evil thoughts?
　　Listen, my dear brothers and sisters: Has not
God chosen those who are poor in the eyes of the
world to be rich in faith and to inherit the kingdom
he promised those who love him? But you have
dishonored the poor. Is it not the rich who are
exploiting you? Are they not the ones who are
dragging you into court? Are they not the ones who

are blaspheming the noble name of him to whom you belong?

If you really keep the royal law found in Scripture, "Love your neighbor as yourself," you are doing right. But if you show favoritism, you sin and are convicted by the law as lawbreakers.[12]

Described here are at least three ways that wealth and power, the two-headed god of this world, can pollute our religion—that is, make our way of living our faith toxic to ourselves and others.

First, James warns us that we are not to show favoritism. Specifically, we must avoid the temptation to prefer rich people over poor people. We're not supposed to suck up to the wealthy, give them special attention or added perks, or give them even more respect than we do to the poorest person present. That's a worldly attitude, and one that can too easily infect us.

How many churches are held hostage by their biggest funder or two? If the personal opinions and agendas of a congregation's wealthiest few outweigh the needs, voice, and dignity of the poorest ones, that congregation's religion—its communal life of faith—has been polluted. How many congregations (or their pastors) resist seriously engaging poor folks because they're nervous about "those people" showing up on Sunday morning and upsetting the middle-class faithful? Pollution.

Missions and other faith initiatives that focus on caring for the poor are, like my Sanctuary community, especially and ironically vulnerable to this tendency to pander to wealth. Such organizations and groups have no money of their own and so have to find support from people with deep pockets, or at least pockets with something in them. They have to walk the tightrope—on the one side is the polluted pit of turning fund-raising into the de facto core mission, and on the other is the dry ditch of not having enough to care for needy people. If we end up tailoring our mission to fit the contrary expectations or requirements of funders, if we follow the money instead of Jesus—pollution!

A fundamental aspect of many church-planting models is the goal of attracting first and foremost the people who are wealthy enough to pay the bills. In order to keep those people, we make sure we have well-equipped worship teams, comfortable seating, state-of-the-art audio-visual gear, and lots of activities aimed at keeping their kids occupied with all the bells and whistles. Of course, those churches tend to be planted in relatively wealthy neighborhoods to make it convenient for the people they hope to attract. See? The perceived need to attract people with money skews the entire approach.

Years ago, I met with such a church planter, who had recently arrived in my city. In the course of our conversation, as I heard about what he hoped to do, my heart began to sink. I encouraged him, as James and others did the apostle Paul when they sent him out as a missionary, "to remember the poor."[13] He responded, "Our church is going to focus on attracting upwardly mobile young people with an intellectual bent. Later, when we're solidly established [financially, he meant], we can reach out to poor people."

Pollution. That meeting took place more than twenty years ago, and to this day that church has not reached out to poor people in any significant ongoing way, let alone seated them in the place of honor in the congregation. Such discrimination, choosing rich over poor, makes us "judges with evil thoughts."

Second, we are to flip the normal standard of our world on its head and live in the reality that God has "chosen those who are poor in the eyes of the world to be rich in faith and to inherit the kingdom he promised." The standard of the world we see everywhere around us is the antithesis of this: Our celebrities are, almost without exception, those who are rich and beautiful or rich and powerful. We have made gods of business moguls, actors, and athletes, showering them with money and adulation. Many municipalities enact bylaws designed to keep people from begging (panhandling) in the city core, where wealthier commuters and tourists might be annoyed by them.

These are the normative sensibilities that Jesus taught us were an illusion and that James, echoing his words, warns us is still more religion pollution. The poor people so disrespected and dismissed by our world are the very people who are smack-dab in the middle of God's world. The Kingdom of Heaven is organized around them. Contrast that with the "kingdoms" of our world, where the wealthy and powerful are protected by police, armies, courts, economic systems, and more, and where, when the poor dare to ask for more, they are immediately categorized as criminals, rebels, terrorists.

Fortunately for me and many others, "rich" people aren't excluded from this Kingdom. We just have to know our place— we must realize and joyfully embrace the fact that we are included on the basis of grace rather than by right. People like me, who have more than they need in goods and public honor, are in the Kingdom of Heaven somewhere on the periphery. Lucky to squeak through the door and rub shoulders with the stars—the orphans and widows.

Not showing favoritism addresses our instinct to rank people—which, if we are being honest, we all do, even though we know it's not right. Recognizing that poor people are at the heart of the Kingdom of Heaven doesn't mean that they rank higher than rich people. (By the way, if you can't imagine yourself saying, "I am poor," just assume you're rich. *Rich* just means you have more than you really need. Ever heard anybody, even someone with tons of money, admit he or she is rich? No, me either.) As James reminds us all, you're supposed to "love your neighbor as yourself." All your neighbors—rich and poor. In general, it may be a bigger challenge for poor people trying to love rich, powerful people than it is the other way around.

The thing is, making sure "those who are poor in the eyes of the world" are at the center of our communal life of faith doesn't ultimately exclude or diminish anyone; what it does is properly orient us to Kingdom values instead of the polluted values of our world. It sets all of us—poor and rich—free to receive the wealth of the Kingdom of God.

This leads us to the third aspect of attitudinal remediation that should engage us: recognizing and dismantling the effect wealth has on people's senses of entitlement and the manners in which they wield the power wealth brings them. Having money and influence isn't the problem, per se. It's what we do with it. James doesn't pull any punches in describing the typical behaviors of people with money:

Is it not the rich who are exploiting you? Are they not the ones who are dragging you into court? Are they not the ones who are blaspheming the noble name of him to whom you belong?[14]

And this is the same kind of person who has come to the church gathering expecting, at least by inference, to have people bow and scrape and lead him or her to the best seat! This is too often typical of people who have grown up with or grown accustomed to the many benefits wealth brings— although in my experience it's by no means always so; I know some truly rich people who are also unassuming, self-effacing, kind, and thoughtful.

Doesn't this remind you of the story of the rich ruler (probably a synagogue official) who came to Jesus wanting to know how he could inherit eternal life?[15] He starts off well, as he runs to Jesus and kneels before him, apparently humble. But it quickly appears that this is mere form, perhaps a way of trying to get his way with Jesus, because when he is questioned about his compliance with the law of Moses, he brushes the query aside: *I've done that since I was a kid. That's not what I'm looking for.* When Jesus pushes the biggest button he has—*give your money to the poor*—the man immediately bails. He has both money and power and so is used to getting what he wants. He can't see that Jesus is trying to set him free from the binding, befouling effect of dependence on money and position. That's what entitlement does; it blinds us and binds us.

James, who was not a wealthy or powerful man himself,

had seen firsthand what such pillars of society could do if someone got in their way. Jesus had lambasted them for putting their religious activities on show and using their position to "shut the door of the kingdom of heaven in people's faces."[16] They tithed in tiny, symbolic amounts but neglected justice, mercy, and faithfulness. "You clean the outside of the cup and dish, but inside they are full of greed and self-indulgence,"[17] he accused them. Pollution.

These religious leaders had so put their faith in money that Jesus ripped them again:

> Woe to you, blind guides! You say, "If anyone swears
> by the temple, it means nothing; but anyone who
> swears by the gold of the temple is bound by that
> oath." You blind fools![18]

It reminds me of the sad "treasure of the church" I saw in Split. Gold, silver, dry bones.

And, of course, it was these very same people who would shortly engineer Jesus' crucifixion. No wonder he commented, as the rich ruler turned around to go, "How hard it is for the rich to enter the kingdom of God!"[19]

We don't know what immediate situations James was referring to when he wrote about exploitation, legal harassment, and slander being directed at early Christians. But it's not really surprising—rich people have employed the same methods for thousands of years to ensure that they keep getting richer and keep getting their way. By and large, they believe they are just getting their due; by and large, those of us who are able to get our way at the expense of others do so. Entitlement wouldn't recognize itself if it looked in a mirror.

On the other hand, two rich men, Joseph of Arimathea and Nicodemus, put the protection their privilege afforded them aside and used their resources to give Jesus a dignified burial while the disciples were skulking behind closed doors. The Ethiopian treasurer, Cornelius the Roman centurion, and Lydia the purple cloth merchant were prominent early converts to the cause of Christ, and all were almost certainly wealthy, at least by comparison to the early disciples. Rich people aren't inherently any more wicked than anyone else. It may be hard for the rich to enter God's Kingdom, but it ain't impossible.

Jesus and James aren't writing rich people off (whew! I have a chance!), but they are warning us to beware the noxious effect of valuing wealth for its own sake, deferring to the people who have it because they have it, and the attitude of entitlement that attends dependence on wealth instead of God.

Placing people who are poor at the center of the community of faith orients all of us, rich or poor, to the true north of God's Kingdom values and keeps our Kingdom work unpolluted.

Along the way, a great many of our theological assumptions and cultural values will be overturned.

The losses in our community come too frequently to ever really finish processing one before another occurs. Grief overlays grief, and it becomes difficult if not impossible at times to know exactly who or what we're mourning. Despite the distance between us, something about Matt's death opened the door of some deep, inner chamber within which I'd been storing up sorrow, anger, and confusion.

I have to admit I didn't like Matt much, let alone love him. He was intelligent and could be charming and energetic—he never had trouble getting jobs, but he could never keep them either—but he was too often destructive, disruptive, disrespectful, and dishonest. He hurt the people who loved him in ways that seemed so casually deliberate that it was all the more shocking. The way he treated a long list of people who had tried to hold him close, who all loved him so well, made me want to punch him far more often than I had any impulse to embrace or even be kind to him. Other folks found ways to care for him, but I'd say I never did. At best, I put up with him.[20]

Yet I found that his death moved me strangely, and not because I felt guilty about my own attitude toward him—I didn't and don't, frankly. I know how human I am. I never had any illusions about being his savior.

I was affected by Matt's death because, if you'll forgive the theological terminology, he was well and truly screwed before he was even born. I don't know how to express it more honestly than that. All you need to know about his family of origin is that he was born with a severe case of Fetal Alcohol Spectrum Disorder (FASD). This left him unable to really empathize, compute the consequences of his actions, understand the value difference between truth and lie, plan for the future, or consistently give and receive any recognizable form of love. And that, as you can imagine, screwed his life—twisted it round and round into a tighter and tighter downward spiral until it came to a final, sharp point.

Steve's family embraced Matt when he was still in high school. They loved him with extraordinary strength and commitment for a couple of decades, and others joined in, but while that love should not have been too little, it was certainly too late. It had always been too late for Matt.

Anyone who knew Matt as an adult could have predicted that he would die early and by one of the typical means in our community. His death was shocking only in the sense that death always is. And that's the splinter that festered in me.

Because how is it just, let alone merciful or loving, that Matt never had a chance? If you say, "Well, Matt still had to make his own choices," I'll respond, "You don't understand FASD." FASD snipped the capacity to make rational choices right out of him as neatly as if it were a surgeon removing an organ. And it did so while he was still in the womb. Where was God in all of this? How are we supposed to make sense of Matt's life and death?

Did his life matter to God or not? Was Matt just a useless bit of excess trimmed off by the great machine that produces the redeemed? *If God loved Matt, how could he stand by and watch what happened to him?*

It made me angry. It's the hurdle I've struggled for years to get over in my relationship with God. He knows I've tried—in the wake of death after death after death and in the midst of the trauma, pain, abuse, and resulting addictions that afflict friends who were or are screwed just like Matt. I know the theological arguments, and none of them satisfy. Yet turning away from the loving and just God I still choose to believe in only makes it worse. It doesn't stop the evil; it only means there is no hope of healing, redemption, or even meaning in the midst of the suffering. So I find no relief in either embracing or dispensing with the theological systems that are supposed to explain such things yet fail so dismally.

I do find some comfort in knowing that, two thousand years ago, Jesus sat on a hillside and preached a sermon about Matt. What he had to say gives me hope that Matt, even now—especially now!—has a great future ahead of him. That he isn't, and never was, disposable or damned from the start. He was never at the bottom at the heap but at the top.

Jesus began to preach that day because the large crowds that had gathered from the surrounding regions included "people . . . who were ill with various diseases, those suffering severe pain, the demon-possessed, those having seizures, and the paralyzed."[21] In short, the crowd included a lot of Matts, plus the people who loved them and had brought them in hopes that Jesus could do or say something to make their loved ones better—people such as Steve's family and others in our Sanctuary community who loved Matt and bore some of his pain with him and kept bringing him to Jesus.

Jesus didn't start out with a funny story or by railing against the injustices of the world. Instead, he cut right to the chase, announcing the Charter of Blessedness—infinitely better than mere rights—of the Kingdom of Heaven. He described what that Kingdom looks like by describing who is important in it. To the surprise of the pain-filled, powerless, demon-harassed people who listened, he described *them*.

In all of my reading of commentary on the Beatitudes, I've never found anyone who went so far as to say this straight out, so I will: What Jesus taught that day means that Matt, regardless of what he believed about doctrinal concepts such as "the person and work of Christ," is a citizen of the Kingdom of Heaven. He was, in fact, thus blessed from the moment of his birth—you could say, in his case, that because he was born screwed, he was also born into the Kingdom and carried the passport all his life, even if he didn't realize it.

Because God *was* paying attention, after all. He knew how apparently hopeless Matt's situation was, knew that Matt was never really going to be "free" to make a choice, and so guaranteed justice, mercy, and love for him in the end and forever. He did so in a fashion that would not, unfortunately, negate the hellish choices others would make, the choices that affected Matt so deeply. Maybe there really is no way to answer that conundrum, and maybe God wishes there were as much or more than I do.

My anger looks for someone to blame and ultimately rests on God himself. God's wrath transmutes through Jesus into a fiery determination that those upon whom every evil force has been concentrated, such that the opportunity of meaningful choice has been negated, will nevertheless see salvation instead of damnation, redemption instead of condemnation, healing instead of ultimate decay, reconciliation instead of banishment, and honor instead of degradation. This is not a get-out-of-hell-free card; this is a key to the city, a last-shall-be-first miracle.

The "person and work of Christ"—his life, death, and

resurrection—makes it possible. The teaching of Jesus in these Beatitudes confirms it. I think that when Matt awoke in the waiting room of eternity and then approached the glorious gate before him, he was recognized immediately and welcomed as a citizen of the Kingdom of Heaven. Nobody checked his passport or inspected his luggage. He wasn't admitted with a kind of grumpy by-the-skin-of-his-teeth acceptance but with what must have seemed to him like inordinate joy, as if his long and difficult war had ended—and he was finally returning home. I would imagine Matt is still wondering how he made it in, if there was some clerical error, and when he'll get booted out.

Soon and very soon, if it hasn't happened already, Someone will explain, "Blessed are the poor in spirit, for theirs is the kingdom of heaven." And Matt, at last, will understand.

the leveling effect

AN OLD PRAIRIE farmer was finally convinced by his daughter, who had long since moved away to British Columbia, to come for a visit. She and her family toured him through the Rocky Mountains, where every bend in the road unveils a landscape more extravagantly and dramatically beautiful than the last. Upon his return home, he was asked by the clerk at the feed store how he had enjoyed his trip. What did he think of the mountains?

The farmer munched awhile on his stalk of flax before answering. "Well, they were nice, I guess," he said slowly. "But they sure do block the view."

When that holy wild man John the Baptist appeared on the scene, he made a phrase from the prophet Isaiah his tagline:

"A voice of one calling in the wilderness, 'Prepare the way for the Lord, make straight paths for him.'"

Luke's account continues the quote from the prophet, explaining what the Lord—the Messiah, as every Jew understood—would do when he arrived:

> Every valley shall be filled in,
>> *every mountain and hill made low.*
> The crooked roads shall become straight,
>> *the rough ways smooth.*
> And all people will see God's salvation.[1]

Every time I read this, it makes me think of the Canadian prairies that defined that old farmer's world. It takes about sixteen hours of driving to make your way across this enormous flatland. Some think it's boring, since the fields of wheat, flax, and canola seem to stretch away, unchanging, into eternity, but it has its own kind of beauty. The pure blue above seems endless. After a while, it begins to feel as though the car is staying in one place, and the brilliant yellow, gold, and purple patchwork of the summer fields are slowly moving toward you, speeding up as they get close, then slowing down again as they slip past and fade in the rearview mirror. The car rises and falls as if on the gentle swell of a calm sea. As if the earth beneath you were sleeping sweetly and breathing slow and deep. Driving westward, you can see a storm coming from a hundred miles away. The driver barely moves the wheel for minutes at a time. Compared to navigating the city I live in, it's effortless.

The Baptist did actually come out of the desert, of course, and the landscape he lived in was nothing like the prairies. Rocky, arid, small little areas of plain enclosed by ridges and rough, lumpy hills and mesas. A trickle of water between the rocks was prized, and a muddy creek like the Jordan was a big deal. For people who walked everywhere—almost everybody in John's day—getting around was a challenge. Up one ridge, down another, around the hill, down the valley, along the dry, stony defile at the bottom . . .

The prairies would have seemed like heaven to any first-century Judean commuter.

But the work of the Messiah wasn't really about getting around physically. This metaphor makes clear that it is about creating access and mobility in the Kingdom of Heaven, leveling the "landscape" so that everyone can move and all can see God's salvation in the distance, rushing toward them, a world-changing thunderstorm of grace. It is about dismantling the hierarchies of wealth and privilege, as well as moral distinction and self-righteousness. It is about chopping the top off the mountain of entitlement and raising up the valley floor of worthlessness.

Michael J. Bryant was thirty-three years old when he was elected for the first time as a member of the provincial parliament of Ontario. His party formed the opposition; four years later, they won a majority, and Michael was appointed the province's youngest ever attorney general.

He had the character and pedigree to be expected in a

political and legal prodigy. His father had been the mayor of the Vancouver Island town he'd grown up in; as a kid, he we small and liable to being picked on, so he took up boxing, a sport that suited his combative temperament. He earned a slew of university degrees, including a master of laws from Harvard (*magna cum laude*); clerked for the Supreme Court of Canada; lectured at King's College London; and became an adjunct professor at the University of Toronto. He practiced law at a firm in New York City and then with one of the Seven Sisters firms that have dominated the Canadian legal landscape for decades—all of this before his political career began.

He would go on to hold other cabinet posts in his incredibly successful ten-year run, including that of house leader, before stepping away from politics to become the CEO of Invest Toronto, a high-profile, brand-new city-owned agency charged with economic development and attracting investment. Most assumed he was seeking distance from a government whose popularity was in decline, in preparation for making his own eventual run for leadership or perhaps a jump to federal politics.

A bare three months later, in a matter of twenty-eight seconds, everything changed. Michael sat in the backseat of a police cruiser, facing charges of "criminal negligence causing death," and "dangerous driving causing death."

The contrast between Michael and the man who had died could hardly have been more stark. Darcy Allan Sheppard was a bike courier; Al, as his friends called him, had spent time in jail and living on the streets. He was handsome and charming, but prone to angry outbursts and, as his adoptive father remarked, had a propensity to make the same mistakes more than once. He was Métis, a people of mixed First Nations and European ancestry who still have to fight to be recognized. Apart from his adoption at age six by Allan Sheppard Sr., who by most accounts seems to be a wise and gentle man, Al never caught a break.

In short, Al was a Sanctuary kind of guy. In fact, he would stop in for lunch sometimes on a Wednesday if a delivery brought him to the neighborhood. His partner hung out in our community and still does from time to time. Like Mike and Matt, he was a Beatitudes person—he'd spent most of his life behind the eight ball, and he was the kind of individual who Jesus said would inherit the Kingdom of Heaven. If you had put Al and Michael Bryant in a lineup and asked anybody in the Sanctuary community who we'd choose for our team, it would have been Al every time.

The case hit the front page of all the local and national newspapers, with every development being reported as a lead item on the evening news. It was more than just a singular tragedy; it had all the makings of a modern-day morality play. An icon of power and privilege, driving home along Toronto's Mink Mile, finds himself in conflict with a street-involved bike courier, and in less than half a minute, the symbol of poverty and marginalization lies dying on the sidewalk.[2]

THE MOUNTAINTOPS DESCEND

In a society in which wealthy people were widely considered to be, upon the evidence, God's favorites, the ones he had blessed, James stands out as one who really didn't have much time or affection for the rich:

> Listen, you rich people, weep and wail because of the misery that is coming on you. Your wealth has rotted, and moths have eaten your clothes. Your gold and silver are corroded. Their corrosion will testify against you and eat your flesh like fire. You have hoarded wealth in the last days. Look! The wages you failed to pay the workers who mowed your fields are crying out against you. The cries of the harvesters have reached the ears of the Lord Almighty. You have lived on earth in luxury and self-indulgence. You have fattened yourselves in the day of slaughter. You have condemned and murdered the innocent one, who was not opposing you.[3]

That's pretty harsh, isn't it? It's as if he began thinking about the guy who showed up flashing gold jewelry and fancy clothes, expecting special treatment, and thinking about it got James mad enough to point out how the rich man's ilk were always exploiting people. Then he let it rest for a bit, but it was still stewing inside of him and erupted again toward the end of his letter, resulting in this lavish tongue thrashing. It's reminiscent of the awful hiding Jesus gave the Pharisees in Matthew 23.

If you're reading this, and you know you have more than enough money, please don't give up just yet. This is just part of the leveling of the landscape. The mighty deluge of grace is coming. While we're at it, may I state, in straightforward fashion, what I alluded to a couple of times in the last chapter? I'm a rich guy.[4] I also have to hear these difficult words—words I can't imagine myself ever speaking to someone else—for myself.

Jesus' suggestion to the rich ruler in Mark 10, that he give away all his money to the poor and follow Jesus, was an attempt to level the hills and valleys in that man's life. As Mark relates the story, just before telling the man to ditch the wealth and power he had come to depend on, "Jesus looked at him and loved him" (verse 21). Jesus' radical approach wasn't prompted by judgment, bitterness, or distrust. He must have known that the chances were slim that the ruler would respond, but his challenge was prompted by love. He wanted to free him from the corrosive effect of the position and material goods to which the man clung.

It's striking that Jesus said, before issuing that challenge, "One thing you lack" (verse 21). The man's dependence on wealth had created a deficit that needed to be filled. The deficit is what James described, in the quote above, in such uncompromising terms.

The more wealth a person has, the more it tends to separate him or her from people who have less. The obvious deficit in this man's life was not having eternal life; he couldn't see that he couldn't have it without also entering into the Kingdom of God, participating fully in the rich life to be found there in a community oriented around people who are poor in spirit, lost in mourning, marginalized by meekness.

> Jesus looked around and said to his disciples, "How hard it is for the rich to enter the kingdom of God!" (verse 23).

Jesus' love for the rich man means we have to hear this comment as empathetic and sympathetic rather than dismissive or judgmental. He knew that all the supposed advantages the man had were only so many hills and mountains blocking his path. His disciples were so surprised by this that Jesus explained, "It is easier for a camel to go through the eye of a needle than for someone who is rich to enter the kingdom of God" (verse 25).

This is an ancient Hebrew joke.[5] The Hebrew language is highly pictorial, and Hebrew humor was rooted in the absurd images the language could evoke. Imagine a cartoon in which a large, gangling, and hairy camel is being pushed through the eye of a needle. A camel's face is pretty funny at any time, but imagine the look on its face while this is happening. For the disciples, this would have been a real thigh slapper. Jesus is treating the issue with a light touch, while still making the serious point that it really is *hard* for someone used to depending on wealth and position to lay them aside and enter a world where the things he or she used to value are almost meaningless.

As far as the disciples were concerned, the rich ruler had everything they wanted for themselves. To them, he looked like a guy who had won God's lottery, so they were astonished by Jesus' insistence on this point. If this champ didn't qualify for the Kingdom, then who did?

Hopeful words then from Jesus: "With man this is impossible, but not with God; all things are possible with God" (verse 27). Even rich, powerful people finding new life in the Kingdom. I imagine Jesus delivered this with the kind of sigh you heave when you tell a joke and your listeners need to have it explained.

It's evident that it took quite a while for this particular penny to drop for the disciples. Luke tells us that, not long after Peter's confession of Jesus as God's Messiah, the disciples were arguing about who would be the greatest—the richest and most powerful, no doubt—when the Master threw out the Romans, restored the throne of David, and began collecting taxes. They were still debating this during the Last Supper![6]

A gospel that teaches and models this is nothing if not radical in the most socially subversive manner. The great work of the wealthy, powerful person who is a citizen of the Kingdom of God is the dismantling of the worldly hierarchies of wealth and power. Poor people can't do this. Only rich people can. To engage in such radical activity is to express in a powerful way the grace that is at the very heart of the gospel. And in doing so they reflect the character of Christ himself, who though he was rich became poor, so that we, who are all poor in comparison to him, might be made rich;[7] who washed his disciples' feet; who explained that the least is the greatest in the Kingdom and that to receive a child is to receive him.

Talk about the mountain being leveled! If we need any confirmation that life in God's Kingdom requires us to relinquish position and privilege, using the resources we've been given to lift up the poor and oppressed, the Incarnation should be more, much more, than enough. If God can become a child and a servant, how can we escape his example? The wealthy, powerful person who is willing to follow Jesus in this way will also find that he or she experiences a surprising side benefit—freedom from the oppression of riches, which we might experience as the insatiable hunger for more, the fear of losing what we have, or the constant weight of managing our material goods. The absurd image of the camel squeezing through a needle's eye no longer applies; dependence on money and position is dismissed, and the lightness of walking freely in the Kingdom of Heaven is the result. This is why James can say,

> The rich should take pride in their humiliation—since they will pass away like a wild flower. For the sun rises with scorching heat and withers the plant; its blossom falls and its beauty is destroyed. In the same way, the rich man will fade away even while they go about their business.[8]

Even taking into account the way rich people seem to get under James's skin, I don't think he means "the rich should take pride in their humiliation" in a sardonic way. The rich person who knows that wealth is, ultimately, fleeting and essentially meaningless, is not driven by the god named More or threatened by the loss of riches because the key to his or her identity is found elsewhere. Managing wealth is not an easy thing; for the citizen of the Kingdom of God, the prospect of being able to lay that burden down one day is something to look forward to.

In the months following the economic crash of 2009, I was struck by the different responses I encountered among my friends. I know a few people who lost hundreds of thousands of dollars within a couple of months, and despite the fact that they were so wealthy that it didn't change their standard of living at all, the experience worried and frightened them. They fretted about it constantly and watched the market reports as if their lives depended on it. Used to being secure in the steady upward march of their net worth, they suddenly felt vulnerable.

By contrast, my poorest friends—who live in sad little rooms or camp under bridges and walk miles every day to get food and clothing—barely registered the crisis at all.

One close friend of mine was, in practical terms, affected by the market's nosedive more than most. He's an investment analyst, and trying to get ahead of trends that proved unpredictable and unmanageable in order to defray the panic of his clients and boss was incredibly wearing. On top of that, his own considerable wealth took hit after hit. And yet, through it all, his greatest concern was not his own portfolio or even those of his clients. It was that his losses would diminish his capacity to give to the work of God's Kingdom. I know him well enough to be convinced that this was not a pose he adopted but rather the true expression of his heart. It was an extraordinary example of one who is not owned by his wealth.

For some, like the rich ruler, the radical surgery of selling all and giving to the poor might be necessary—and well worth it!—to save the life of the soul. But Jesus also offered another paradigm. After dinner one day at the house of a prominent Pharisee, he took the host aside and gave him a lesson in Kingdom etiquette.

> When you give a luncheon or a dinner, do not invite
> your friends, your brothers or sisters, your relatives, or
> your rich neighbors; if you do, they may invite you back
> and so you will be repaid. But when you give a banquet,

invite the poor, the crippled, the lame, the blind, and you will be blessed. Although they cannot repay you, you will be repaid at the resurrection of the righteous.[9]

Here is a way that the wealthy person can become free of the ego traps and expectations and obligations that stick like leeches to piles of money. Use it to bring in the people who are welcome nowhere else, and lavish on them the riches of the Kingdom. Feed them, heal them, empower them. Raise them up. Give them the seat of honor. Make them your people. Use your resources to bless, without seeking repayment in the obsequiousness of supplicants or the accolades of your social peers, and you will be blessed.

Live this with a child's dependence and vulnerability, and a servant's submissive humility and dedicated energy, and you will look more like Jesus every day.

Cyclists, social activists, and especially bike couriers across the city staged rallies and made plain their fear that, given his connections, the case against Michael would be whitewashed. Mr. Sheppard pled with Al's angrier friends not to take the matter to the streets, while also decrying the way his son was summarily dismissed in some quarters as a troubled man bound for a bad end and thus dispensable. Journalists took sides, interpreting the known facts in a widely disparate manner, then reinterpreting them as further information came to light. Most, predictably, seemed to take a barely disguised delight in the fall of one who had been high and mighty. The irony was so delicious that the tragedy often seemed obscured.

The same ministry of the attorney general that Michael had once headed now brought in a special prosecutor from out of province, in a bid to avoid the appearance of favoritism, to assess the validity of the charges and if necessary to pursue them in court. Michael resigned his position with Invest Toronto and hired both a public relations firm and a lawyer famous for representing wealthy clients in deep trouble. To some, these moves served as an early tacit confirmation of his guilt.

There could be little doubt on which side the instinctive sympathies of our community placed us. Possibly subverting those sympathies was what might be described as the natural empathy of ones who themselves come from places of privilege: My own origins are much more similar to those of Michael than those of Al. In some ways, it was temptingly easy to grant Michael an assumption of innocence that most of our core community members could not. Privilege, as surely as poverty, has its own set of pathologies.

But the Kingdom of God is not about taking sides. It is not about judging guilt or innocence, nor is it about embracing "our kind" to the exclusion of anyone else. It may be harder for a rich person to get into heaven than for a camel to squeeze through the eye of a needle, but as Jesus also remarked, "With God all things are possible."[10]

Jay Barton, although he is a member of Sanctuary's staff, spends more time in Michael's world than in Al's. He raises a good portion of the money that funds Sanctuary's staff and a wide range of activities. Perhaps more than anyone else in our community, he is engaged in trying to bring the "mountain-tops" down to where they can meet the rising "valleys." That's the Kingdom agenda, really, and the necessity of fund-raising is the mechanism. We're not all that interested in merely sticking our hands into deep pockets and raiding the wallets we find there. We want to introduce wealthy, powerful people to Kingdom community because we think they need it too.

And so, in spite of our instinctive sympathies, without regard to Michael's guilt or innocence, and in the midst of the media storm that raged around the case, Jay reached out to Michael. Not to ask but to offer; he knew Michael was hurting and suspected he would also have found himself suddenly and dramatically isolated. It was true, of course: Michael had become political Kryptonite, and the most his friends and previous associates could afford was the occasional supportive text message. His marriage, already in trouble, would flounder under the strain within a year. Not long after that, Michael's brother would die unexpectedly. His world was spinning. And by now, it was public knowledge that he had for a few years been in recovery from his own addiction issues.

At first, Jay met Michael for breakfast, for coffee, just to talk. After a while, he invited Michael to come to a drop-in meal, where I met him for the first time. He seemed on edge to me, full of nervous energy and in constant motion. He came, I think, expecting that he would get to "volunteer."

I don't remember it, but Michael says I told him to just go over there and sit down. Eat, relax. Introduce yourself and talk to somebody. Pass the bread when you're asked, and clean your plate off when you're done. He says I said nothing then about kinship or love or leveling. Nothing about Jesus. He waited until I wasn't looking and snuck out.

THE VALLEYS RISE UP

"Believers in humble circumstances ought to take pride in their high position."[11] What an astonishing statement, right near the beginning of James's letter! Why would a person who is at the bottom of the heap in spiritual or social condition (that's what "humble circumstances" means) take pride in it? Boast about it, glory in it? And how is it that his apparently low condition is actually a heavenly one? That's a better translation for "high position": a position "on high," in the sense of "in the heavens."

It's beginning to sound like the first Beatitude again, isn't it? "Blessed are the poor in spirit, for theirs is the kingdom of heaven." Except here, James is also saying that the brother or sister should know that he or she is so blessed and should make a big deal out of it.

If knocking the tops off the mountains of wealth and power is part of the Kingdom equation, then raising up the valley floors of poverty and oppression is another. Maybe the idea is that the mountaintops are tumbled into the valleys to level things up, like a spiritual version of a landfill. The sum of this leveling equation is justice—God's Kingdom justice.

Some readers will already be thinking that all this leveling sounds dangerous. You're not alone. Many years ago now, I preached at what was then my home church, a conservative middle-class suburban congregation. The text I had been assigned was the latter part of Acts chapter 4, which describes the revolutionary and euphoric early days of the church. Part of the text says, "All the believers were one in heart and mind. No one claimed that any of their possessions was their own, but they shared everything they had."[12]

As was usual in that church, I went to the back of the auditorium when I was finished speaking to greet the members of the congregation as they exited. One older man, a solid blue-collar worker all his life, squeezed my hand a little tighter than usual, gave me a piercing stare, and grumped, "It sounds like communism to me."

If your inclination is similar to his, I will give you the response I gave him: It's the Scripture you're arguing with, not me. Both Isaiah and John the Baptist made it clear that this was fundamental to the mission of the Messiah, and the very early church made every attempt to live it out accordingly.

And anyway, it's not communism. Communist dogma justifies the violent overthrow of the wealthy by the poor, then forces the redistribution of wealth by communist government mandate. And, of course, it denies the authority and dismisses the example of Jesus, our King.

In the Kingdom of Heaven, by contrast, the rich willingly bow down and the poor rise up because both recognize Christ as King and one another as brothers and sisters. They do so joyfully, discovering results similar to what that same passage in Acts observes: "With great power the apostles continued to testify to the resurrection of the Lord Jesus. And God's grace was so powerfully at work in them all that there were no needy persons among them."[13]

Do we really want to be able to testify with power, with *great* power, to our resurrected Lord? Do we long for the pouring out of his grace on ourselves and our communities? Then this is how we will live the gospel. This is what true religion looks like. We live out what we really believe, not just what we say we do.

We cannot afford to interpret the gospel of Jesus Christ according to political convictions or social conventions we have absorbed from the culture around us. We must submit our politics and habits and fears to the rule of the King. To do otherwise is to choose as our ruler the god of this world.

It isn't easy for someone who is used to being lowly to embrace his or her blessedness. Our wealth-and-power-addicted society tends to demean, marginalize, vilify, and even criminalize people who are poor. Because they are vulnerable, those who aren't tend to victimize them further.

A story told by Jesus illustrates both the very different attitudes of and the spiritual implications for people who are at the apex of society and those who are at its foot. It starts out like a joke: Two guys go up to the temple to pray . . .

. . . one a Pharisee and the other a tax collector. The Pharisee stood by himself and prayed: "God, I thank you that I am not like other men—robbers, evildoers, adulterers—or even like this tax collector. I fast twice a week and give a tenth of all I get."

But the tax collector stood at a distance. He would not even look up to heaven, but beat his breast and said, "God, have mercy on me, a sinner."

I tell you that this man, rather than the other, went home justified before God. For all those who exalt themselves will be humbled, and those who humble themselves will be exalted.[14]

The man who evidenced such a lowly opinion of himself wasn't likely even a financially poor person, because tax collection was usually a lucrative business. His form of "poverty" was social shame—his profession and its association with the Romans made him an outcast. The high-flying Pharisee judged him at a glance: *Thank God I'm not like that guy!* We might do the same for this or other reasons: race, choice of clothing, adherence to another religion, level of intelligence, degree of social grace, sexual orientation, differing politics, and so on. We are co-opting the values of the world we live in materially instead of internalizing the values of the Kingdom where our spirits have citizenship.

James calls this "friendship with the world" and equates it with fooling around on God:

> You adulterous people, don't you know that friendship
> with the world means enmity against God? Therefore,
> anyone who chooses to be a friend of the world
> becomes an enemy of God.[15]

James goes on a bit about submitting ourselves to God instead of fighting for and among ourselves—we'll look at that more closely in another chapter—and then paraphrases Jesus' summation of the Pharisee-and-tax-collector story: "Humble yourselves before the Lord, and he will lift you up."[16]

This is why "believers in humble circumstances" have an

advantage worth celebrating: They're already low enough—aware enough of their own needs—that God can lift them up.

If we are to live a Kingdom life together, those among us who are used to being in charge will want to get out of the way of people who are in materially humble circumstances, making space for them, recognizing and affirming their rightful place at the heart of the Kingdom of Heaven, and making sure they hold a position at the center of our communities of faith. Those of us who are in fact poor will want to be obedient to God by embracing the blessedness of our current social condition and fearlessly stepping forward to claim our place at the center of a Kingdom in which we will have enough materially and untold wealth spiritually. Finding ways to do this in real life, in real-time ways, is how we can participate in the Messiah's work of raising the valley floor. We'll want to find ways to come down off our mountaintops, too, so that we also can get low enough to be lifted up. Valley dwellers and mountain dwellers need to move toward one another. It's those of us who are wealthy who usually have the greater distance to travel. Gravity, at least, is on our side.

Remember Jesus' counsel to the man who put on the gala dinner for Pharisee bigwigs? *Next time, invite the rejects.* Step out of your gated community (whether material or spiritual) and meet the real world. Encounter the Kingdom of God.

Such a dinner was not being proposed by Jesus as a mere act of charity on the part of the wealthy man. Really, he was describing what Kingdom community looks like: not a bag lunch but a feast, a banquet where everyone knows they are welcome because those sitting in the place of honor are the ones who are normally not welcome anywhere else: "If even *those* people are welcome, surely I must be welcome too!"

This is part of the point of James's warning at the beginning of chapter 2 about doing the normal thing and giving the place of honor to people who are wealthy and successful. If we do that, we'll find eventually that the church is made up mostly of people who are, relatively speaking, wealthy and successful. In fact, this is what we actually have done in the Western world, in general, and that has been the result.

In a 2007 study, the Barna Group reported that, although almost three of four people in the general population believe that poverty is one of the most serious social problems facing the States today, evangelical Christians were only half as likely to believe the same thing.[17] Followers of Jesus have become too comfortable and far too insular. We might even say that we have ceased following Jesus and are now following one another, nose to tail in a downward spiral.

A true Kingdom community is one in which privileged and disadvantaged people operate as partners, pooling their resources as the infant church did. By choosing to become communities where rich and poor live their lives together and share what they have—power and vulnerability, food and hunger, self-sufficiency and humility, opportunity and opposition—we'll find that the need of one is met by the resources of the other. The rich will discover surprising places of poverty in their lives, and the poor will discover that they are rich in ways they never dreamed. Together we'll discover, along the way, that some things we thought were deficits are actually positives, and vice versa; that both can be the locus of redemption at work in our individual and communal lives.

We've been experiencing this in the Sanctuary community for a long time now. When we eat together (at least a couple of times each week), the people who do most of the cooking, serving, and cleaning up afterward are what we call "core community members"—men and women who are street involved, homeless, or minimally housed, often struggling with the usual facets of street-level poverty. They are the hosts. When we worship, the most powerful, prophetic voices among us come from the same folk. When well-meaning middle-class people call us wanting to volunteer, we say, "You can't. All those positions are filled by our core people. But you're more than welcome to visit. We'd love to serve you a meal and give you the chance to get to know our people!"

We bring wealthy people in to visit too, because we believe they also need an opportunity to engage with the Kingdom of God in action—and, of course, because we need their money. Successful entrepreneurs, corporate leaders, senior bank executives, construction moguls, political figures, and a Supreme Court judge have all stopped by. Inevitably, the most effective advocacy they'll hear, both for Sanctuary and for the broader cause of justice, will come not from Sanctuary staff members like me but from core community members who are clearly "Beatitudes people." Unprompted, those members approach these powerful visitors and testify to their own personal experience of redemptive Kingdom community. Almost without exception, those visitors remark on the vitality and positive vibe they sense in a room jammed with a hundred or so of the city's poorest and neediest people.

The wealthy among us have discovered that we need our poor brothers and sisters at least as much as they need us. As our core community members—who are used to being told a thousand different ways, "You have nothing anybody needs"—learn the truth of this, they gain dignity, and the valley is filled in just a little.

THE REDEMPTIVE AGENDA

Just after tearing his second strip (of three!) off rich people, James puts relations between rich and poor people in perspective:

If you really keep the royal law found in Scripture,
"Love your neighbor as yourself," you are doing right.
But if you show favoritism, you sin and are convicted
by the law as lawbreakers.[18]

Favoritism shouldn't be shown in either direction. While poor people are at the center of the Kingdom, their place there doesn't exclude rich people—it merely reorients all of us to the larger purpose of Kingdom justice. The point is to discover one another as neighbors and love accordingly.

The leveling effect we've been discussing is, I believe, an expression of the goal of God's redemptive agenda. Paul expressed it beautifully and concisely in his letter to the Galatians:

In Christ Jesus you are all children of God through
faith, for all of you who were baptized into Christ have
clothed yourselves with Christ. There is neither Jew
nor Gentile, neither slave nor free, nor is there male
and female, for you are all one in Christ Jesus.[19]

The cross of Christ dispels every distinction of race, social
condition, or gender. This is the spiritual reality toward which
we are trying to live, in a world full of systems, hierarchies,
and cultural attitudes bent on maintaining those barriers.
Our job is to dismantle them, not because we think we'll ever
complete the assignment but because it's how we testify to
the goodness of the King who owns our allegiance. It's how,
together, we experience his grace and his presence and live
out the salvation that is at work in us. Along the way, we may
just find that we are turning the world upside down.

This is the shining beacon in the darkness that draws us
onward. We're not there yet, but we can dream. And more than
dream—we can live it. Here. Now.

Michael Bryant kept coming back because, as uncomfort-
able as he was entering the environment, he discovered he
felt better when he left. The idea that he might develop some
friendships had never crossed his mind, but that's what
started to happen. Frank, a gruff older guy who looked like he
could still bench-press two-fifty, stared him down a few times
but then started waving when he saw Michael walk through

the door. They would talk politics and social justice together, Frank pulling from his bag articles he'd clipped from papers and underlined in red pen. Frank's conversational mode was all Socratic method—question after probing question fired in an aggressive tone; the lawyer in Michael loved it. Louise[20] flirted with him and asked him regularly if he was married—a friendly, running joke.

It was complicated, having Michael in our community. Frank later told Michael that he'd gone red in the face for three days when Al had died—but now he was glad to see Michael. Many of our staff members were apprehensive about having him around. We had questions about what it meant, in such a situation, to stand on the side of justice. Michael had recently been at the head of a broken, often unjust legal system that is especially oppressive to people who are poor and afflicted with addictions and post-traumatic or other mental health issues. First Nations and Métis people, like Al, are incarcerated at a far higher rate than any other segment of our society. We didn't want to be seen as giving the rich man the place of honor and telling the poor man to shove off. We worried especially about Al's partner and a few other bike couriers who still frequented our drop-ins. Would they feel safe and cared for? Would they believe, even in a community like ours, that their needs would be placed before those of someone who was wealthy and powerful? Could they even speak up if they didn't?

We warned Michael that we were committed to the Beatitudes people first, and we asked if he would be willing to sit down for a mediated meeting with anyone in the community who had a beef with him or who just wanted to say something to him. He agreed readily, knowing he might be setting himself up for some very painful encounters. We did our best to work it out with each of the community members who we thought might have a personal stake in the matter, and we discovered that although they weren't keen to hang out with him, neither did they feel the need to drive him out or tear a strip off him. Al's partner was especially gracious but still uncertain that the concerns of a single mom on welfare would be balanced equally against those of someone like Michael. The net effect, though, was that they made a wary space for him. Talk about the valley floor rising up.

It would be a mistake to think that any of this has been perfectly resolved. The prosecutor eventually withdrew all charges, noting that there was no reasonable prospect of conviction, that Al had been in a rage, and Michael was legally justified in the attempt to get away, which resulted in Al's death. Still, years after the fact, some journalists and activists continue to argue that there should have been a trial. Mr. Sheppard, while stressing that he is not seeking vengeance or a retrial and doesn't even object to the dropping of the charges, nevertheless believes that his son didn't receive justice—that some evidence was dismissed or ignored because of who Al was and who Michael was. There were nineteen witnesses, he claims, whose testimonies were not considered at all.

This is the kind of tension we have to live with when the leveling effect of the gospel brings the rich and poor into close personal contact, into the same community. It's not just a theoretical or cultural tension, nor does it all weigh on the poor people, who usually do bear the brunt of any such conflict. It's real, immediate, relational, and no respecter of persons.

One day, a year or two after Michael had started hanging around in our community, I received a phone call from him, and he was seriously rattled.

He told me he'd been riding his bicycle—yes, his bicycle—north from the downtown core. A southbound bike courier glanced across the street at him, and Michael saw the man's eyes bug out. He'd clearly been recognized. As they passed each other, Michael thought, *Uh-oh, there goes a guy whose day has been wrecked. He'll spend the rest of it wondering what he should have done or said to me . . .*

Four blocks later, the courier had chased him down and blocked his way.

"Why are you profiting from Darcy Sheppard's death?" he began screaming. "How do you live with yourself, murdering someone and then exploiting his death?"

The man ranted further about the book Michael had written about his experience, about the Son of Sam law and Michael's evil character. Michael realized the courier was filming the entire interaction on his cell phone. They were stopped beside a café patio; Michael turned to the patrons and shrugged, trying his best to defuse the matter. The courier ran out of other things to say and contented himself with simply shouting "Murderer!" over and over.

Despite his appearance of equanimity, Michael felt as if his blood pressure was going to blow the top off his head. A succession of crazy thoughts bolted through his mind: *Fight back! Smack that phone out of his hand. Last time you tried to get away—how did that work out? Maybe you should get violent. Hit him! Throw the bike at him!*

But when he opened his mouth, something unexpected and entirely different came out.

"I think I'm supposed to pray for you right now," he said, half to himself.

The courier stopped yelling for a moment, gaped, then hopped on his bicycle and rode circles around Michael while screaming "Murderer!" once more. Finally he rode off.

I thought it was interesting and encouraging that after this unnerving incident Michael immediately called me, rather than one of his socioeconomic peers, for support. And it made me chuckle to hear him describe with wonder this new instinct to pray in the face of persecution. Michael, it seemed, was orienting himself more and more as a citizen of the Kingdom—discovering that, although he was wealthy and powerful, in some deep sense he belonged among those who were anything but.

He says now that when he first began to visit our community, the world seemed very small. He was depressed, full of self-pity, and quite paranoid, worried that he would be recognized and made a target of people's anger. He was prepared in his own mind to be a hero or a martyr—evidence, he says now, that he was fixated on himself and the narrative he was creating.

New friends such as Iggy began to change the game for him. Ig would joyfully announce events that wouldn't have seemed like good news to most: He'd gotten a room! He'd gotten his stolen TV back! Michael admitted that it felt so good to be his friend. Frank, too: "You gonna be here next week? Good, I got some more articles for you." Each time he visited, Michael stayed a little longer. Eventually he stopped thinking about himself and started thinking about the people he was talking to. Slowly he realized that few knew who he was, and nobody cared. "It was a great leveler"—his words.

"Friends, family, comfort." Also his words. Who'd have thought this legal and political prodigy would find that in a community like this? Today he's a practicing legal aid lawyer, defending people with mental-health and addiction issues. He's living the gospel.

"I don't go to Sanctuary to be helpful or charitable," Michael says. "I go to feed my soul."

He remembers going to a community concert. The band played, a wild mix of people danced and sang with a joy that seemed inordinate, and Michael sat off to the side, drinking it in. He was feeling great, feeling like he belonged for the first time. As he was leaving, he overheard Alan Beattie— Sanctuary's executive director—and Jay talking. They were discussing a couple of street-involved community members whom Michael had met, just checking in on how they were doing. Then he realized with a start that they were now talking about him. "How's Michael? How's *he* doing?"

"It cracked me open because I realized they regarded me like everyone else," he says. "They were looking out for me! It felt like an honor to be an equal there—it felt like a gift. It filled me up. I felt like the Grinch in that scene at the end of the movie, where his heart that used to be too small swells up. It changed my life. More than the accident."

watch your mouth!

IF YOU HAD TO put your finger on one thing that defines bad religion, what would it be? I'd guess that most people would choose one of two basic categories: hypocrisy (saying you believe one thing but doing another) or toxic dogma (beliefs that sanction or encourage you to speak ill of or even do harm to others). Both, unfortunately, are easy targets.

Examples abound of people who laud purity but cheat on their spouses, present themselves as honest while cheating on their taxes, or go on about the riches of God's grace while cheating the waitress of a decent tip. Let's face it, all human beings are, to some degree, hypocritical. None of us lives perfectly to the standards we set for ourselves, regardless of our religious or nonreligious beliefs.

Identifying religious beliefs that actively support destructive activities isn't very difficult either: suicide bombings, gay bashing, flagrant disregard for our belabored environment, the subjugation of women, racism, slavery, lynching, and even war.

Surprisingly, with so many lurid options to choose from, it seems like the first thing that came to mind for James was people who talk too much: "Those who consider themselves religious and yet do not keep a tight rein on their tongues deceive themselves, and their religion is worthless."[1]

You have to like James, don't you? He doesn't sugarcoat anything. If your mouth keeps running away with you, no matter how you talk it up, you aren't living the gospel. Honestly, when I think of all the stupid things I've said through the years, this makes me shudder.

As far as James is concerned, how and what we communicate is a critical facet of how we live out our faith. It's a theme he gives lots of attention, returning to it several times in the course of this short letter, with a different approach each time. His first mention is as follows:

My dear brothers and sisters, take note of this:
Everyone should be quick to listen, slow to speak
and slow to become angry, because human anger
does not produce the righteousness that God desires.
Therefore, get rid of all moral filth and the evil that is
so prevalent and humbly accept the word planted in
you, which can save you.[2]

"Take note of this," James says. Pay attention! This may not sound as if it's all that important, but it is. When we keep talking instead of listening first, we're usually just trying to carry our point. We want to convince others, and maybe ourselves, too, that we're right. When we're challenged, it touches our ego, and we get angry. Not infrequently, we convince ourselves that anger is justified—we're right, after all, and others should be able to see that! James calls this kind of attitude "moral filth" and "evil that is so prevalent" (or "abounding wickedness"[3]). No, he's not pulling any punches.

And no wonder. It's this kind of attitude and approach that has led to innumerable factions and splits within the church. We talk so loudly and continually that we stifle the growth of the implanted word, the voice of God's Spirit whispering within us, and rush to defend our own vision of the way things ought to be instead of God's. What we say steers us, one way or another.

When we put bits into the mouths of horses to make them obey us, we can turn the whole animal. Or take ships as an example. Although they are so large and are driven by strong winds, they are steered by a very small rudder wherever the pilot wants to go. Likewise, the tongue is a small part of the body, but it makes great boasts.[4]

There is some good news in this for us. If we listen first—for that quiet word God has planted in us and for that same word in what others have to say—we may be able to speak healing instead of wounding, blessing instead of cursing, liberation instead of domination. That would be steering the ship in the right direction. We don't have to boast and then defend the boast, insisting on the fundamental "truth" that we are right and others are wrong. Any boast, really, is a way of saying "I'm bigger and better than you." And that is the seed of conflict.

The anger produced by such conflict begins to drive still more conflict, and an anger fed is an anger that grows. "Human anger does not produce the righteousness that God desires." It can't. *Righteousness*, remember, is Kingdom justice in the context of relationship. Righteousness seeks the good of the other; how can that happen if what we really want to do is insist that our own opinion carries the day?

Kingdoms have been divided, wars have raged, families have been broken, individuals have been harassed, murdered, and even executed by the state, all in the name of Christ. Microcosmic versions of the same thing have taken place within denominations (which are themselves a result, in the first place, of this very matter), local churches, and families. No wonder James writes, a little later,

> Consider what a great forest is set on fire by a small
> spark. The tongue also is a fire, a world of evil among
> the parts of the body. It corrupts the whole body, sets
> the whole course of one's life on fire, and is itself set
> on fire by hell.[5]

It makes you wonder, doesn't it, what sort of nasty things people had said to James through the years? It certainly reminds me of the incredible vituperation I've encountered myself when my course or convictions have differed from those of individuals who feel qualified to sit in judgment. When a Christian comes to you and says, "Now, I feel compelled by love to say this to you . . ." you know you're up to your hips in the stinky stuff. The fire of hell is licking at your toes. And not because the condemnation that's coming is necessarily accurate—James says it's the tongue that speaks with such disregard for the gracious, patient, quiet voice within that carries that sulfurous reek.

In exactly this sort of situation, Jesus quoted Isaiah to some Pharisees, whose habit was so clearly to listen and watch only enough to be able to accuse:

> These people honor me with their lips,
>   *but their hearts are far from me.*
> They worship me in vain;
>   *their teachings are merely human rules.* . . .
>
> You have a fine way of setting aside the commands of
> God in order to observe your own traditions![6]

They talked a good game but were so determined to prove the rightness of their understanding of God's law that they had stopped listening to the Lawgiver.

Many of us do the same. It's as if we say to ourselves, "Well, God doesn't seem to have much to say to this person/situation/issue. I better set him/it/the matter straight myself." As James points out, we can tame all sorts of wild animals, but we can't tame our own poisonous tongues.[7] They don't just poison others; they poison us, too. Jesus, expanding on his challenge to the Pharisees, said a little later to his disciples,

> What comes out of a person [what they say and how
> they act] is what defiles them. For it is from within,
> out of a person's heart, that evil thoughts come—
> sexual immorality, theft, murder, adultery, greed,
> malice, deceit, lewdness, envy, slander, arrogance
> and folly. All these evils come from inside and defile a
> person.[8]

Wow. It's quite a list, isn't it? This is the poisonous fruit of listening only to our own internal talk, the loud voice of *Me! Me! Me!* that chokes out the tender word that has been planted within us.

The story told by Jesus about a wealthy man with all kinds of intelligent but selfish plans illustrates this perfectly. His land had produced a bumper crop, and like any good entrepreneur, his first thought was expansion. Tear down the barns and build bigger ones. That would lead to increased wealth and security for many years. He looked forward to taking life easy: eating, drinking, and being merry. Throughout the anecdote, the man's ongoing interior monologue is related to us: He's talking himself into a good, sensible business plan that leaves God out. But God's plans were different: That very night, the man would die.[9] Although the main point of Jesus' story was a warning against greed, it also shows how dangerous it is for us when, instead of listening first for God's voice, we drown it out with the needy, grasping chatter of our own souls.

When we speak without first listening intently for that implanted word, we reveal that we don't really want what God wants for us. We want what we want for us, and we're not above using religion, let alone pragmatic business plans, to get it. This is how James describes it:

> What causes fights and quarrels among you? Don't
> they come from your desires that battle within you?
> You desire but do not have, so you kill. You covet but
> you cannot get what you want, so you quarrel and
> fight. You do not have because you do not ask God.
> When you ask, you do not receive, because you ask
> with wrong motives, that you may spend what you get
> on your pleasures.[10]

Who is king in this kingdom, anyway? Based on the evidence of the way many of us live, and much of the history of the church, it isn't Jesus. The wars that have been fought over competing Christian dogmas or between "Christian" nations (God save us!) is at the larger end of the scale of this dangerous, toxic religion. Those people who talk about receiving a call or a word from the Lord as a means of justifying what they want to do themselves, often without regard to how it will affect those nearest them are, perhaps, at the smaller end.

It seems ludicrous to even have to point it out, but merely attaching God's name to our own plans or points of view doesn't actually sanctify them. You would never know this by listening to some who claim to follow Jesus. It's hard to escape the impression that more than a few Christians view God as a kind of celestial rubber stamp on their own opinions and intentions. They want everything they do and say to have *Approved by God* stamped across it, nice and clear, so others can read it. Wouldn't it be simpler and much more honest to admit that we're mostly not sure? That we're walking by faith, not by sight? That we're relying on God's grace and mercy rather than our own ability to get it right?

I wonder if our proclivity for attaching this kind of phony seal of heavenly approval to our own junk was what James had in mind when he wrote, *"Above all, my brothers and sisters, do not swear—not by heaven or by earth or by anything else. All you need to say is a simple 'Yes' or 'No.' Otherwise you will be condemned."*[11]

Truly following Jesus looks very, very different:

To you who are listening [you who listen first and not so that you can figure out how to destroy my argument, but so that you can really understand] I say: Love your enemies, do good to those who hate you, bless those who curse you, pray for those who mistreat you.[12]

Now that's how we can live out the word that is growing within us.

––––––––––

We at Sanctuary wondered in early days, *How do we enact this Kingdom agenda in real-time, practical situations? If people who are poor and usually excluded are truly supposed to be at the center of all, what are the middle-class white folks like us supposed to do about it?*

The situation in our community was and is not like that in many very poor countries, where a $300 microloan will buy a sewing machine that can provide income and the beginnings of a business to support an entire family. Money, while important, was often the least pressing of the needs of our people, who struggled with post-traumatic and psychiatric conditions, addictions, and much more. Men and women who were usually not able to care well for themselves were not going to be able to care well for one another, were they?

Just take community meals. Who would plan the menu, do the shopping, cook the food and serve it, and clean up afterward? It was a challenge for sure, but slowly we began to realize that what we thought of as "serving" was often a matter of retaining power and control for ourselves—our competent, efficient selves. In a soup line, after all, who has the most power: the one shuffling along with a bowl on a tray or the one holding the ladle?

We could see the essential indignity of it. Despite our constant assurances that there was more than enough food for all, people began to line up half an hour before the food was served. Many would take their food to a table, bolt it down, and hurry back into line. They spent more time standing like cattle in a pen than they did eating. If submission to God meant, for those of us who were rich by contrast to others in the community, releasing our power and control so that "the poor" could assume their rightful place, how were we actually supposed to do that?

A soup line was not how we had begun. Originally, I had begun to invite the odd individual or small group of people

I met on the street to come back to Sanctuary, where there was an old-school church kitchen we could use to make some lunch together. Grilled cheese and soup one time, spaghetti the next. Then grilled cheese and soup again. Simple. We'd sit and eat it at the old wooden table with the retro Formica top. We had zero culinary range, but the food filled the hole, and it was nice to sit there together. Things got more complicated as more and more people showed up. Ultimately, we devolved to the more efficient soup line format, with a few competent and reliable volunteers doing the work. It sucked the soul right out of it.

Still, when it was suggested that we deliver platters of food to the tables and let people serve one another, I objected.

"They'll never share it evenly," I said. "The first few people who serve themselves will clean the platter off, and there'll be nothing left for the others at the table." I could foresee fights breaking out.

The day we first tried the new approach, we made, I was sure, another tactical error: We served roast beef, a rarity in church basement drop-in or mission meals because of the cost. We had agreed that we organizers, once the food was delivered to the tables, would sit down and eat alongside the rest of the diners.

When I was finished hustling around, I plopped myself down in a seat at the end of one of the long tables, eight diners to each. I served myself some mashed potatoes and mixed vegetables—there wasn't a lot left, but enough—then sat waiting for the meat platter to make its way to me. When it arrived, it held the serving tongs and one miserable scrap of beef about the size of my thumb.

Ha! I thought. *I knew it! This will never work.*

I was still rehearsing my arguments with grim self-satisfaction when I heard a kind of grunting coming from the opposite end of the table. Looking up, I met a pair of eyes lasering their way through a thicket of hair and above a tangle of beard. I didn't know who the man was, and I don't know that I ever met him again. He had a massive slab of beef on his fork, and it was dripping gravy all over the table as he waved it in my direction. He grunted again and gave the beef an extra little jiggle. It was clear what he meant. He'd checked up and down the length of the table and seen that I had gotten shortchanged.

Oh, I thought. *Oh. This* will *work after all.*

LISTEN LONG; TALK SHORT

There's a story in Acts 15 that illustrates the challenge of listening carefully for God's voice and then communicating together circumspectly. It begins with some authoritative types going from Judea to the Syrian city of Antioch, where Paul and Barnabas had been preaching. It seems that, in their lofty opinion, Paul and Barnabas had been missing a vital point: Believe in Jesus all you want, they said, but "unless you are circumcised, according to the custom taught by Moses, you cannot be saved."[13] So there. These are the rules, we've always done it that way, and therefore it must be so. (Furthermore, that's the way we like it. Those upstart Greeks will have to become Jews if they want to join the club.)

Paul—the ex-Pharisee—and Barnabas had been down this particular road a number of times before, and they were pretty sure these Judean theologians had it wrong. It's hard to imagine Paul in particular as one who would back down from an argument, but instead of slugging it out with them, he and Barnabas meekly went to Jerusalem, the cultural and spiritual heart of Judaism, to try to sort it out with mature help.

It didn't go well at first. As soon as they reported what they'd been doing in Antioch and elsewhere, they met the same objection. There were Jerusalem believers who were also Pharisees (seems like there still are), who echoed the ones who had gone to Antioch, pronouncing, "The Gentiles must be circumcised and required to keep the law of Moses."[14] Circumcised *and* required to keep the law! It was getting worse.

After a lot of discussion, Peter got to his feet. He told the story of how God had, some years before, chosen him to speak to the Gentiles about the gospel. When he had done so, he said,

God, who knows the heart, showed that he accepted them by giving the Holy Spirit to them, just as he did to us. He did not discriminate between us and them, for he purified their hearts by faith. Now then, why do you try to test God by putting on the necks of Gentiles a yoke that neither we nor our ancestors have been able to bear? No! We believe it is through the grace of our Lord Jesus that we are saved, just as they are.[15]

There's more to the story, lots more, but let's just pause there a moment and notice that Peter—bold, impetuous but highly respected Peter—listened carefully to the Pharisee believers and all the discussion that followed before talking himself. That, I think, was a Peter who had learned a thing or two about the dangers of speaking first, fast, and loud.

He didn't tell the whole story of his mission to the house of Cornelius, the Roman centurion, that day, but James and at least a handful of the others had heard it earlier, complete with the embarrassing details.[16] You remember this passage from Acts 10, I'm sure: Peter, praying on the rooftop patio of the tanner Simon's house in Joppa, falls into a trance. He sees "something like a large sheet being let down to earth"[17] from heaven, and within the sheet are all kinds of four-footed animals, reptiles, and birds.

Then he hears a voice: "Get up, Peter. Kill and eat."[18]

A shocked Peter replies, "Surely not, Lord! I have never eaten anything impure or unclean."[19]

"Do not call anything impure that God has made clean."[20]

It happens three times, and by the last, I imagine the voice has a little growl in it. Peter is still wondering what all this means when Cornelius's emissaries arrive. The next day, they travel together to Caesarea. When Cornelius prostrates himself at Peter's feet, Peter shows that the message is starting to filter through.

He says, "Stand up. I am only a man myself. . . . You are well aware that it is against our law for a Jew to associate with or visit a Gentile. But God has shown me that I should not call anyone impure or unclean."[21]

As Peter listens carefully to Cornelius describe how God has been speaking to him, it sinks in deeper still. When he has heard everything Cornelius has to say, he responds, "I now realize how true it is that God does not show favoritism but accepts from every nation the one who fears him and does what is right."[22] And he continues on to share with the entire household the amazing Good News of peace through Jesus Christ.

It is nothing less than a revolutionary moment, both in Peter's life and in the history of the church. Peter, who was so prone to respond with a quick "Surely not, Lord!" to anything that didn't fit his preset parameters of understanding, has learned to listen until he understands, and he is able to discern the quiet voice of God.

He shows the depth of that learning later in Jerusalem. The old Peter would likely have leaped to his feet to shout down the Pharisee Christians who hadn't had his experience. He would have dominated the ensuing conversation, using the weight that his status as number one disciple gave him. He might have moaned loudly, "Oh, please—we've been through all this before!" Instead, he listens and listens some more, and then speaks with humility. Beautiful.

Almost as sweet is the example set by James, our James, who by this point had become the acknowledged leader of the Jerusalem church. In early church tradition, James was referred to as James the Just, because he cared so deeply about God's justice for people who were oppressed and poor, and because he was known to be careful and evenhanded in decisions he made regarding the church. His patient, wise listening is on display in this account.

He, too, listened that day to the concerns of both Paul and Barnabas, and the Jewish fundamentalists. He listened silently to the long discussion afterward and to Peter's response. Then he listened some more while Barnabas and

Paul told about the miraculous wonders God had done among the Gentiles through them. At last, when everybody else had finished talking, James spoke up:

> "Brothers," he said, "listen to me. Simon [Peter] has described to us how God first intervened to choose a people for his name from the Gentiles. The words of the prophets are in agreement with this. . . . It is my judgment, therefore, that we should not make it difficult for the Gentiles who are turning to God."[23]

He had listened to the voices, one by one, of everyone who spoke that day. He recalled the voices of the prophets, who nobody else seems to have referenced. He heard the internal voice of God and concluded that God isn't interested in making things difficult for people, but in drawing them to himself. When the people in Antioch read the letter relating the decision to which James had guided the group, they "were glad for its encouraging message."[24]

Communication is a group activity. Talking without listening is a way of telling God or other people that they don't matter. Ultimately, it means that we're talking only to ourselves or the people within the circle who say the same things we do. How small will we draw that circle?

Imagine if followers of Jesus were known as people who listened first and long and talked later and short. Imagine if others knew that we were people who brokered agreement instead of splitting into factions, that we held our tongues because we really want to understand rather than clamoring to make our point. Imagine that we had a reputation for making things easy for people instead of insisting that they follow our rules, our values. What if we admitted, as Peter did, that God often has to speak to us several times before we actually begin to hear him? And we changed our perspective and approach when we do?

Wouldn't we look and sound more like Jesus?

THE KITCHEN REVOLUTION

The kitchen is the heart of any home, and at Sanctuary it's no different. It makes sense, then, that the endeavor to enact the Kingdom characteristic of submitting the needs of the wealthy—who are so adept at getting and keeping what they want—to those of the ones who are usually denied and marginalized would begin there. But this is a quiet, patient revolution; it has continued and will continue to work its way through our community, for there are many miles to go before we will arrive at our destination.

For those whose voices are usually the loudest and most authoritative, being slow to speak and truly listening to those who are usually ignored or dismissed is another characteristic of the submission to which our Lord calls us. This submission means continuing to love when love is hard or even when love is not reciprocated. It will mean letting go of judgment—our tendency to want to discern the difference between the wheat and the weeds,[25] between who's in and who's out.

This, too, is a path to joy, although it may even mean that we sometimes end up suffering a measure of persecution, either from people whose own traumas prompt them to harm others, or from the powers we have formerly aligned ourselves with. What we trust, ultimately, is that there will be healing for all.

A few years after the Roast Beef Revelation, Donald became our kitchen facilitator. Donald was living in a men's shelter when he first came to Sanctuary, dragged along by a small posse of dedicated boozers who could see that the big man needed somewhere to belong. Having our people serve one another the meal had led quickly to having them cook it, and Donald found his way into the kitchen in no time at all.

That's about when we began to talk about "core" members of the community: the Beatitudes people whom God intends to be right at the center and to "anchor" members—the privileged and (usually) more stable people whose proper role was a more peripheral supporting one. We began to see that we needed to protect, wherever possible, the actual work being done at Sanctuary from middle-class volunteers, as their participation in this way tended to supplant the involvement of our core people, who were used to being shoved out and told their efforts were unnecessary, unwelcome, inadequate.

By the time Donald became a member of our staff, he was both core and anchor in our community. He now calls himself a facilitator rather than a manager because, he says, having found his way to the center himself, his real job now is to make sure that others on the margins get involved. Don's crew of mostly street involved people now cooks and serves about twenty-five thousand meals each year to their street-involved friends and a handful of more privileged people for whom Sanctuary is also home.

We still have a lot of "wealthy" visitors to the community. Some come because they've heard about Sanctuary somewhere and want to see it in action. Others are seminary or social-work students or, increasingly, younger adults who want to follow Jesus in the real world. Routinely, Jay brings others like Michael Bryant—wealthy, powerful, influential people from the high-pressure worlds of business or government. Some arrive more than a little nervous, like the former Supreme Court judge who whispered to Michael, "Were you afraid when you first came here?" The people who welcome them and make them feel at home are people such as Carlo, Angela, Matt, or Traci: street-involved members of the community who have come to "own" the place. They can and do, often without knowing it, articulate beautifully to these visitors (and certainly more powerfully than I can) what the Kingdom looks like and how they've experienced it for themselves.

The people who used to be shoved out have found a home, a place within a large, very dysfunctional family. They're claiming their inheritance and generously welcoming others, even the rich and powerful. And some of those people find a home with us too.

CHAPTER NINE

the surprise in submission

IT MAY BE THAT the more extreme manifestations of bad religion that we've noticed so far are not, these days, the main reason so many are turning away from a public, communal expression of faith that engages the world we live in.

Simple boredom may be a more potent factor. Sports events are more exciting. A rib fest or a day at the beach is more exciting. A movie you've seen before is often more exciting. Frankly, most things are more exciting than our usual experience of church life, which for nearly all of us means, mostly, church services that many of us attend out of a sense of duty and perhaps longing. It may be that we're getting religion in doses just weak enough to inoculate us against desiring more and to anesthetize us into the bargain.

This anesthetizing effect is what Karl Marx had in mind when he famously labeled religion as "the opium of the people."[1] He meant religion was the "drug" that poor and oppressed people used to deal with the pain of their lot in life. Put your head down and just keep slogging; don't question your betters; your life might be nasty, short, and brutal, but it will all be worth it when you get to heaven. Marx was convinced that religion was just one more chain among the fetters the wealthy and powerful used to keep the "proletariat" enslaved.

Richard Dawkins, Christopher Hitchens, and other atheist apologists have expressed the opinion that religion encourages people to stop thinking, to keep them from seeking more knowledge of the world and universe around them.

They make good points, don't they? For hundreds of years in Europe, most of our ancestors lived in grinding poverty. They gave to the "nobility" everything except a small portion to keep themselves alive, on the specious grounds that God had placed those nobles above the lower orders. Until the 1960s, African Americans were fed the same stupefying gruel by the purveyors of a whites-first perversion of Christian religion—despite the eloquent cries of prophets such as Sojourner Truth. Martin Luther King and others came along and began to flip the temple tables over, but the virus of that pernicious don't-get-uppity dogma still rages in the veins of the body politic in the form of white entitlement and obtuseness, and the resulting, often necessary, black reaction. The resistance of those of us with an evangelical heritage to matters as diverse as climate change and accessible health care for people who are poor indicates that some of us at least are eager to keep believing what we've always believed, and what's comfortable for us, rather than being challenged to think more broadly and perhaps having to admit that we haven't always understood God perfectly and completely. Such an admission might actually cost us something. There must be thousands of other examples of the ways we often choose false religion over true, and our miserable little idols over the living God.

The subject of submission to God, which is so important to James and such an obvious requirement of really living out our faith, seems at first glance to play right into the attitudes I'm criticizing: Don't try to change things; just trust that God will look after everything. Don't try to understand things; just follow the rules and trust that God knows what's going on. Submission is just not a popular concept in our time, if it ever has been.

But if we were truly submitted to God, we would do what he says we should. We would be set free from the miserly constraints of a me-first culture. We would strike off the chains of oppression, challenge and refuse to bow to any authority that is contrary to his, place the poor rejected ones at the center of church and society, eagerly share our possessions instead of making rapacious capitalism our economic model, seek unity over defending our own points of view, love the people who hate us, trust God instead of guns, vote according to Kingdom principles instead of self-interest, cultivate servants before leaders, and trade vengeance for forgiveness. Instead of being the opium of the people, true religion would be our adrenalin. We would revolutionize the world.

We would seek hungrily to learn everything we could about God and the universe he has created, never being threatened by the possibility that what we have previously understood might be mistaken. We would find that the more we learn, the more we realize how small our learning is; the boxes in which we have kept our tiny understanding of God would expand until they blew apart. We'd be thrilled by this process, eager to shed our ignorance and live in a wider landscape of faith. We'd find we know him better, even as we discover how little we really know about him or his incredible, wonder-full creation. Our understanding of God would be revolutionized.

Isn't this true? Isn't this what we're actually supposed to be? The reality is that we can't live a true, lively, muscular religion unless we trust God enough to submit to him.

The people to whom James was writing were being severely tested in this regard, and James didn't shy away from it. Nor could he, since his letter was addressed "to the twelve tribes scattered among the nations"[2]—Jewish people who lived outside of Palestine. This seems to indicate that he was writing at a time when the church was still mostly Jewish and that they were not "scattered" as a matter of choice, but by other forces. It seems most likely that he was addressing the followers of Jesus described at the beginning of Acts 8, who were driven out of Jerusalem by the persecution surrounding the murder of Stephen, himself one of the first deacons of the church.

James wasn't just talking theoretically, then, when he wrote,

Consider it pure joy, my brothers and sisters, whenever
you face trials of many kinds, because you know that
the testing of your faith produces perseverance. Let
perseverance finish its work so that you may be mature
and complete, not lacking anything.[3]

It's radically counterintuitive, isn't it? Our usual response
to hard times is to feel as if things have gone wrong and to pray
that God will fix them. If we're feeling particularly faith-full,
we manage to trust that God must have some larger purpose
in this awful situation or that he'll redeem it somehow, and
we hunker down to wait it out. We would be inclined to put
joy at the end of this equation, not the beginning—once we've
arrived at the maturity that results from persevering through
trial, we'll be able to, maybe, feel some quiet joy in it. From a
distance, say. When it's over.

But James says we should embrace joy in the middle of it.
Pure joy. This is some radical kind of submission to whatever
God is doing! Depending on your theological perspective, you
may think that God actually sent those trials into your life or
that he merely allowed them. Either way, to actually revel in
the challenge of it, to rejoice in the sense that *God is at work
here!* is a mode most of us find difficult to adopt. Most of us
probably don't even think, really, that we should adopt it—
God should fix it!

But that's only because we're not submitted to God's
agenda in the first place. If we are going to become the kind
of fully enfleshed, Spirit-breathing army that Ezekiel saw
God raise up from a valley full of dry bones, it won't be easy.

We may not be driven from our homes and hunted down (although we might), but committing ourselves to the battle for Kingdom justice will certainly lead us into some dark, bloody corners.

Although I came from a highly privileged family and have continued to live a privileged life by most socioeconomic standards, sharing that life for most of my adult years with people who are desperately poor in almost every regard has tested my faith deeply. The pat doctrinal answers of my youth were exposed as hollow, powerless. My heart, like the hearts of my brothers and sisters in the Sanctuary community, has been repeatedly broken by death and violence within the community and by the diabolically oppressive forces from without. At times, it feels as though all we can do is to put our heads down and take one more step forward, weeping as we go.

But. Strangely. *There is joy in the midst of it.* I don't know how to explain this, but it's true. A kind of joy that I've never experienced among the trappings of wealth, a sense of God's companionship I've never known in a conventional church service. The testing of our faith in this sort of context ultimately leaves us no option but to either pack it in and slink away or root ourselves more deeply in God. Many of the things we used to think we knew have been trimmed away, but our God grows bigger, and we grow more fruitful.

Jesus spoke about this rootedness, the painful pruning, and the surprising fruit of joy to his disciples in the upper room.

I am the true vine, and my Father is the gardener. He cuts off every branch in me that bears no fruit, while

every branch that does bear fruit he prunes so that it
will be even more fruitful. . . .

I am the vine; you are the branches. If you remain
in me and I in you, you will bear much fruit; apart
from me you can do nothing. . . .

As the Father has loved me, so have I loved you.
Now remain in my love. If you keep my commands,
you will remain in my love just as I have kept my
Father's commands and remain in his love. I have told
you this so that my joy may be in you and that your
joy may be complete.[4]

This rootedness, and the joy that results, is dependent on
obedience to his commands. Submission. The submission of
a branch to the vine that feeds it. A submission that compels
us, as Jesus would go on to say, to love one another and even
lay down our lives for one another, just as he did for us. It
means we are taking on the character of the one to whom we
submit. These are not merely euphemistic or poetic phrases;
they characterize the demanding reality of really living what
we believe.

Neither should we fool ourselves that this manner of living
will be easy or at least grant us great clarity regarding all the
things we wonder about. Remember the cry of Jesus on the
cross: "Why have you forsaken me?"[5] Our faith will be tested
to the point of questioning whether we really have any idea at
all about what God is doing. James assures us, however, that
we'll receive the wisdom we need for the situation:

If any of you lacks wisdom [what do you mean *if*, James?], you should ask God, who gives generously to all without finding fault, and it will be given to you. But when you ask, you must believe and not doubt, because the one who doubts is like a wave of the sea, blown and tossed by the wind.[6]

God gives wisdom, not relief, from the trial itself. Enough wisdom to keep persevering, growing, maturing. Becoming, ultimately, who God made us to be. Not doubting—not thrown around by worries that maybe God isn't paying attention or that the obstacles in our way must mean we're on the wrong path.

Listen: Faith is not required when things are going the way we want them to. Faith is for hard times. Doubt is the soil in which real faith grows.

James returns to the matter of perseverance a few verses later, echoing the last of the Beatitudes: "Blessed is the one who perseveres under trial because, having stood the test, that person will receive the crown of life that the Lord has promised to those who love him."[7] The crown referred to is an athlete's reward, sort of like an Olympic gold medal, and here it appears to also be a recognition of the love that compelled the perseverance.

Wanting to clarify that God isn't being unfeeling or mean toward people who actually love him, James continues by pointing out that temptation isn't the same as trial.[8] It doesn't come from God, for one thing, and it doesn't come from without—its source is our own hungry souls. As Jesus said, "All these evils come from inside and defile a person."[9] God is interested in refining and strengthening us, not tripping us up. We can trust that God's gifts will always be good, and his purpose in giving them is to cultivate us into being the cream of the crop.

It's good to remember that, because we're tricky enough to turn our own internal struggle to submit to God into battles with other people. Psychologists call it transference, and it's a very handy little skill—if I make my problem your problem, I can blame you for it instead of having to deal with it myself. Not my problem! It's distressingly common not only in interpersonal relationships but also within the large, dysfunctional family that is the church.

> What causes fights and quarrels among you? Don't
> they come from your desires that battle within you?
> You desire but do not have, so you kill. You covet but
> you cannot get what you want, so you quarrel and
> fight. You do not have because you do not ask God.
> When you ask, you do not receive, because you ask
> with wrong motives, that you may spend what you get
> on your pleasures.
>   You adulterous people, don't you know that
> friendship with the world means enmity against God?[10]

Most of the battles within the early church were fought over competing dogmas or at least with those dogmas as an excuse. It's not much different now, except that usually we don't kill one another over it anymore. Historically, that's a fairly recent nicety. We've already seen that James had to deal with these kinds of scraps, and Peter apparently got so battered by them that at one point he lost track of which side he was on.[11] Often, the people leading the charge are noisily insisting that they understand God accurately, and the reprobates with the contrary view are either ignorant or heretical.

It could be convincingly argued that nothing has done more to damage the cause of Christ than disputes of this sort—that the greatest impediment to the gospel is and has been the various levels of dysfunctional relationship within the church. This is the church drunk on its own power, wielding doctrine like a sword, bent on the domination of people's lives, on empire and the glory of its leaders. This is the church that has submitted God to itself, instead of itself to him. There's only one antidote:

> Submit yourselves, then, to God. Resist the devil, and
> he will flee from you. Come near to God and he will
> come near to you. Wash your hands, you sinners,
> and purify your hearts, you double-minded. Grieve,
> mourn and wail. Change your laughter to mourning
> and your joy to gloom. Humble yourselves before the
> Lord, and he will lift you up.[12]

Submission to God. Only by submitting to him can we resist the devil, and so see the old snake cut and run (or slither). Resisting the need to be right, to be powerful, to be comfortable—the desire, in a phrase, to be my own God: the one temptation that underlies all temptation. Submission to God is the one weapon that works against the devil and his arsenal of temptations, and it's the one path that leads us closer to God.

So "wash your hands"—change what you do. "Purify your

hearts"—change what you desire. Focus your will on one thing: God. "Mourn" the losses that have piled up because you, because *we*, have so long lived according to our own agendas—personal losses, communal losses, global losses. Our nutrition-starved souls, our shallow churches, the gaping wounds between nations, religions, cultures, races, the rich and poor. Instead of seeking to anesthetize yourself with a trifling happiness, "humble yourself before the Lord" of heaven and earth, and allow him to exalt you with a mighty joy.

Submission to any other would be a constraint. Submission to God, a submission that must require us to live his gospel with abandoned hearts, sets us free from the paltriness of this present world, its poisonous confections and mean conceits.

> Now listen, you who say, "Today or tomorrow we will go to this or that city, spend a year there, carry on business and make money." Why, you do not even know what will happen tomorrow. What is your life? You are a mist that appears for a little while and then vanishes. Instead, you ought to say, "If it is the Lord's will, we will live and do this or that."[13]

This submission may begin with a moment of soul-naked prayer, but if that prayer has any meaning at all, it will change the way we live each day. We will raise the All-Sufficient God[14] above the god of self-sufficiency. His priorities and agenda will become ours. We will not seek to dictate the time line. The practicalities of life will not disappear, but submitted actively to the will of God (that is, to his Kingdom agenda as well as his moving in our individual lives), they will be reordered and imbued with a meaning and portent that will be greater than we can know.

As we begin to live lives together that seek the advance of the Kingdom of Heaven here and now, the expression of its radical justice in and salvation for our groaning world, we will inevitably become impatient. How could we not, when we hear the cries of people we have come to love—people who are lost, hungry, oppressed, excluded, humiliated, or even dying? Our eagerness to see them, and ourselves, relieved and lifted up will become like a growing hunger within us, a hunger to experience the blessedness that God says is ours as a banquet instead of an appetizer. We may even become angry that the Kingdom is so slow in coming. There is, I think, a kind of holiness to such impatience, hunger, and anger.

Nevertheless, we will have to be patient. Even as our hearts cry, "How long, O Lord?" we will have to

> be patient, then, brothers and sisters, until the Lord's coming. See how the farmer waits for the land to yield its valuable crop, patiently waiting for the autumn and spring rains. You too, be patient and stand firm, because the Lord's coming is near.[15]

Patience in the face of the urgency of the needs we will encounter as we seek to live the true religion of Jesus may turn out to be the highest form of submission. We work, we pray, and we wait for the Lord to come and begin the harvest. I don't know when he will come in glory, at the end and beginning of all things, or what it will look like when he does.[16] But I know that any ripe heads of grain that may be gleaned here and now arc also dependent on him coming near. I can't be trusted to tell the difference between weeds and wheat, but he can.[17]

This I also know: When he does come in glory, he will say to those who live it,

> Come, you who are blessed by my Father; take your inheritance, the kingdom prepared for you since the creation of the world. For I was hungry and you gave me something to eat, I was thirsty and you gave me something to drink, I was a stranger and you invited me in, I needed clothes and you clothed me, I was sick and you looked after me, I was in prison and you came to visit me. . . .
>
> Truly I tell you, whatever you did for one of the least of these brothers and sisters of mine, you did for me.[18]

"You hate me, Greg Paul," Iggy spat. "You know you do. I can see it in your eyes."

He was a bit high. I'd had to remove him from a community meal because he'd been threatening someone else, but I knew that wasn't why he accused me of hating him. He'd begun to behave like this almost routinely of late. I'd also discovered that it was fruitless to try to respond when he was in this kind of mood. No words I could offer would dissuade him from reciting these awful words over and over.

An Ojibwa man in his forties with a scraggly mustache and a jaw deformed by having been broken and never properly set, Iggy and his family of origin had seen the worst of First Nations experience in Canada. Children scooped from their families in previous generations and delivered to white residential schools where physical and sexual abuse was rife, for no reason other than they were native. Poverty, addiction, and violence on the northern reservations. Frequent early deaths of friends and siblings. More physical and sexual abuse.

Iggy was a clear-eyed and acerbic critic of the white culture that had, with the collusion of government, church, police, and courts, systematically destroyed his people and continued to ignore or oppress them. He was also a brilliant tattoo artist and addicted to heroin.

I stood still, watching him silently while he paced a step or two in either direction on the sidewalk and kept spewing his accusations. We both knew what he was saying wasn't true. We'd been friends, good friends, for a long, long time. But what he was saying wasn't just words, either. It meant something. Still, it wasn't easy stuff to listen to; I wanted to shout him down, call out the lies, challenge or accuse him in return.

A couple of years earlier, I had found Iggy in the alley between Sanctuary and the tall condo next door, overturning garbage bins, kicking the trash around, and swearing frantically. I had no idea what had triggered him; he seemed uncertain of where he was. I yelled at him to stop, but it was as if I weren't even there. When Iggy went for yet another bin, I lost what little patience I'd had.

After stepping up behind him, I slipped my arms under his

and lifted him off his feet. While he wiggled and kicked furiously, I carried him across the alley and away from the bins. It may sound more impressive than it was: In recent years, illness and the junk had shrunk him to skin and bone, and it felt a little like carrying a large and lively bird. I dropped him, only a matter of inches and onto his feet, but his legs crumpled beneath him and he collapsed in a heap on the concrete. He was weeping now, cursing himself and beating his own head on the ground.

It was far from my proudest moment: Picking up the garbage after he had run out of steam would have been easier and less destructive to his already battered self-image. In the months that followed, I heard hints and rumors that I had beaten Iggy up that day. They came from Iggy himself, apparently, and while they gained me some modest and unwanted street cred with a very few, it puzzled me. Why would he say that? I had at least lifted and carried him as gently as I could. Most of the guys on the street will deny someone else has beaten them even if it's true. It didn't seem to affect our relationship—if anything, we seemed to be better friends than ever.

We had had lots of good times between that day and this night, punctuated every now and then by episodes like this one. Wild accusations that I hated him, had put a hit out on him, couldn't wait to see him dead; threats, too, which, though extravagant, were as essentially ridiculous as the accusations. I stood there looking him in the eyes whenever possible, keeping my mouth shut and my face expressionless.

He shouted a couple of times, angry, inarticulate yelps, then stumbled out into the street and lay down in the middle of it. This had happened before too; I knew trying to move him or persuade him to move would only make him more determined to stay there, so I turned and went back inside the building. Without an audience, he would soon get up and off the street.

Over time, I began to hear, in Iggy's bitter words and outlandish actions, the perverse voice of self-abnegation. He told me I hated him because he thought I ought to; he beat his head on the ground because he thought that was what he deserved; he told others I had beaten him because he wanted it to be true—he thought he deserved that, too.

It was tempting to be dismissive of some of his childish actions, such as lying down on the road, or to take personally the vile things he sometimes said to me and others in the community. I will admit that there were moments when I did want to beat him—or at least to give him a good spanking.

But when we got our own egos out of the way, we began to hear the words behind his words. When we took into account his own tragic story, including the wicked, lasting infection in the soul caused by childhood sexual abuse, we began to interpret differently.

Iggy began to come to our Sunday worship gathering. He'd slump on the floor, or sometimes on a chair, just inside the entrance, with his hoodie pulled down over his face. Sometimes he would rock back and forth, bumping his head on the wall behind him.

Every now and then he'd turn his face to the ceiling. He'd cry out to God in the same terms and tone he'd yelled at me, "You hate me! You've always hated me."

"Where were you when . . ." he'd say, then go on to describe in graphic language some of the horrors he'd experienced as a child. "I'm just another drunk Indian who'd be better off dead."

It wasn't easy to receive what Iggy had to say or to hold him at the center of our community. His ranting was disruptive and deeply disturbing, hardly typical language for a church service. We knew, though, that this was one way we could love him—by listening as he wrestled with God. Submitting to the awful sound of a soul at war with itself, convinced that it deserved to be hated and abandoned by its Creator but longing, hoping against hope, that forgiveness, healing, and reconciliation were possible.

He wasn't trying to be a nuisance. It was evident that he was, in fact, wrestling, and with an honesty that was terrible to hear. He kept coming back, kept speaking out loud the nature of his torment, and as he did, some of us began to realize he was speaking the language of our own fearful hearts.

Could God really love us? Could we love one another? Did we deserve it? Could we be forgiven? When a child's body is being abused, his or her soul being blighted, how could God's love and his absence be reconciled? Dare we truly trust? What hope was there if we didn't?

There was no verbal answer to Iggy's questions and our own that would satisfy. In the end, the only response that mattered was loving him and one another.

As time went on and Iggy's body weakened, he seemed to find some healing for his soul. He became softer, less tortured. He no longer hurled those heartbreaking accusations and spoke more and more frequently with affection of his many friends in the community—wealthy white folks like me, as well as his street-involved First Nations brothers and sisters.

One day I stopped in at Lucas House, one of the community homes that Sanctuary facilitates. I discovered Iggy visiting there, stretched out on a couch, watching TV. He had taken to stopping in, sometimes overnight, if he felt too weak to make it all the way back to his own place. My business with the other residents was brief; I concluded it and made my way to the door, stopping to rest my hand briefly on Iggy's head and say good-bye.

"Greg," Iggy called as I opened the door. "I love you."

It was the last thing he ever said to me. He'd been saying it to me and to many others in the community for months. A week later, I was on the other side of the world, preparing to give a devotional followed by a day's worth of teaching to a conference of Australian Salvation Army officers, when I received the news that Iggy had died. He had slipped into a coma on the evening of the day I had seen him at Lucas House, and he never came out of it.

I had been following his situation via e-mail and knew that he had been attended by a rotation of his friends—poor, wealthy, native, white, Sanctuary staff, worshipers, and street people—around the clock every day throughout that long week. In the evenings, they jammed the Intensive Care Unit waiting room, going in to visit two at a time. When his mother and son arrived from way up north, Iggy's Sanctuary family made room and held them, too.

At the end, the medical staff removed the life-support systems and trundled the machines out of the room to make space for the crowd that jammed around his bed. James Smith, an unofficial elder in our community whose own life experience has mirrored Iggy's in many respects, was there. So was Michael Bryant. So were a dozen others who loved him, and there was Iggy, who had loved them, at the center. I'm told his passing was a profoundly holy event, and I, for my part, can hardly imagine a more powerful expression of the body of Christ.

In Australia that morning, I felt as lonely and homesick as I ever have in my life. I desperately wanted to be with my people, but here I was on the far side of the globe, doing, I supposed, what I was supposed to do. It didn't feel like it. I couldn't imagine how, in about half an hour, I would stand before those good people, who were just now finishing breakfast, and come up with anything at all to say.

The conference center was situated around a tiny lake in the midst of the Snowy Mountains south of Canberra. My room had a small balcony that hung out over the lake; I stepped out onto it, searching for a full breath.

There over the far end of the mirrored water, splitting the clouds and brilliant in the morning sun, hung a perfect rainbow.

a twenty-first-century reformation

THE WORSHIPERS HAD, in ones and twos, slipped from among the crowds and carts on the Appian Way, out of the bright August sun into the cool darkness of the catacomb of Prætextatus. They knew that there were informers among them, but what could they do about that? Not much, really. Pray for them, love them, and hope that God would convert them. The effort at secrecy was in any case largely for form's sake—parading boldly and publicly to a gathering of the church would seem like arrogance to the imperial officers and was certain to draw a harsh response. For a time, there had been a tacit understanding that as long as the Christians were circumspect, they would be left largely unharmed. Even the Emperor Valerian's edict of persecution the previous year—forbidding among other things the gathering of Christians in the catacombs, on pain of death or exile—had gone mostly unenforced. This catacomb was a smaller, less obvious one than that of Callixtus opposite. Perhaps that had helped.

Sixtus sat, as usual, on a chair to speak to the gathering. Disciples crowded around him in the small antechamber and sat where they could in the stone niches beside the piles of bones, jamming the narrow passageways spoking away from the entrance. Sixtus spoke quietly, but his voice projected clearly through the catacomb, echoing faintly and reaching easily even those farthest from him. Before him, on a rough block of stone draped with a piece of cloth, were the cup and the bread.

He had not yet raised the bread to give thanks for it when a sudden metallic clatter and a shouted order at the catacomb's mouth announced the arrival of soldiers. Sixtus sighed heavily and appeared to offer a brief silent prayer heavenward before struggling to his feet. Gently parting with his hands the bodies that had closed tight around him, he began to move toward the entrance. Four of his deacons followed immediately; Lawrence hastily removed the Communion cup and, after pouring the wine out on the ground, hid it beneath a nearby mound of skulls. Then he followed.

Sixtus and the deacons stood blinking in the sunshine before a small detachment of the urban cohort. The soldiers had not even bothered to enter the catacomb, knowing that the leaders of these Christians would deliver themselves up in strangely polite fashion. The head of the troops stood patiently and easily with his hand on the hilt of a sword that remained in its sheath.

"Sixtus?" he asked. The pope nodded. "You will die today, old man."

He did not say it unkindly. He unrolled a small scroll and held it up, but Lawrence noted that he did not actually look at it. Probably unable to actually read it. As he recited the emperor's new edict, disciples at the back of the crowd—many still in the catacomb itself—began to moan. Stripped of the officious language, it announced that bishops, priests, and deacons were to be summarily executed and that all their property as well as that of the church to be seized.

"Which one of you is Lawrence?" the soldier asked. Lawrence pushed between the handful of people in front of him to stand at the shoulder of Sixtus. The commander turned to his troop, pointed at two soldiers, and waved them out of the rank with his hand.

"This one goes to the præfect," he said.

As the two soldiers moved forward, Lawrence threw his arms around Sixtus and burst into tears.

"Father," he moaned. "Where are you going without your deacon?"

"I am not leaving you, my son," Sixtus answered, patting the younger man's back. "In three days you will follow me."

It was a long, dusty trudge back toward the heart of the city with his hands loosely tied behind him. A soldier held the other end of the rope, giving an absentminded jiggle every once in a while as one might with a dog. The soldier and his mate joked and chatted together, ignoring Lawrence entirely.

They passed a wineskin back and forth at one point but offered none to their prisoner. Lawrence was glad—it at least gave him time to dry his tears and regain his composure. Still, there was only one possible end to this, and he wondered if he was ready.

They passed the Temple of Saturn at the base of the Capitoline Hill and then the ancient and enormous Temple of Jupiter. It was late in the afternoon when they arrived at the præfectoria and ascended its broad steps. Within the colonnaded patio at the top, the soldier holding Lawrence's leash jerked him to a stop. The other disappeared within. He was gone a long time, returning with a fierce little man in a fine toga. The soldier holding the leash had utterly ignored Lawrence until this, but now he kicked the backs of his prisoner's knees and forced him to the ground.

The little man stared a long moment at Lawrence before speaking.

"You are Lawrence, archdeacon of these Christians?" he barked. "You have control of the purse of your cult? It is forfeit, by edict of the emperor. You will deliver it, and all the deeds of property, and all the items of fine cloth and precious metals and gemstones you and your acolytes have hoarded. If you do this swiftly, your life may be spared."

Lawrence looked up, his mouth open with astonishment. He stammered, plucking at the breast of his homespun tunic, a poor man's garment, and tried to explain—the church owned little, had no property beyond a few scrolls, some lamps, a cup used by all for its ritual . . .

The little man—the præfect, evidently—glared at the soldier who held the leash.

"Hit him," he ordered. The soldier gave Lawrence a mighty whack across the back of his head with the end of the rope.

"My informants tell me otherwise," the præfect snapped. "They tell me that in your meetings—your illegal meetings!—you and the others go on and on about the great riches you have. You will gather these riches and bring them here, and you will do so quickly. No doubt you have hoarded this treasure to avoid taxation, and now you will forfeit it all."

Again Lawrence tried to explain, but he had barely begun to speak when the little man's face began to redden.

"Your fellows have faced the tribunal, and their heads are already in a basket!" he roared. "Including the two—" he searched for the word—"deacons who were not at the catacomb. You see? I know all about your disgusting little band. Do not test me further. The treasure. Now."

They had not suffered, then. That itself was such a relief that the absurd notion of a church that had to meet in a bone-filled cave possessing treasure began to strike Lawrence as funny. His heart calmed, and he met the præfect's eyes.

"It will take some time," he said. "Will you grant me three days to gather the treasure and transport it here?"

The three days were busy. It was true the church owned no property in the sense of buildings or land, but they did have some items: scrolls—valuable only to followers of the Christ; a substantial purse—already in Lawrence's care as the deacon who organized the care of the poor; and the hidden cup. The cup itself had some small value, as it was an antique made of beautifully turned agate, but it was truly precious because generations of disciples of Jesus had drunk Communion wine from it. Some said that Peter had brought it to Rome and that it was the cup that the Lord himself had passed among the disciples at the Lord's Supper.

The cup he retrieved from the niche where it lay beneath the bones, wrapping it in the cloth that had been pulled from the stone that had served as a Communion table, and that still lay crumpled on the ground. A soldier or two may have been ordered into the catacomb to search for treasure, but the inspection had obviously been brief—they were a superstitious lot, soldiers, and while they might easily stroll the bloody aftermath of a battlefield, they were not inclined to linger among caves of the dead. Lawrence jotted a letter of explanation and farewell to his parents and entrusted both it and the cup to a friend who promised to carry them back to Huesca.[1]

Then he made a circuit of the slums, walking slowly lest the small bags of coins he had hidden beneath his robes begin to jingle and attract the pickpockets and cutpurses, and then delivered these coins to people in need. He visited widows and orphans, beggars, broken old soldiers, the saddest prostitutes of the quarter, and men and women who were blind, lame, or even mad. He reminded each of the love of God, the sacrifice of Jesus, and the Kingdom he had taught them would be theirs. He encouraged them to be faithful to God and to care well for one another in their need, especially in view of this new wave of persecution that was beginning. And he made a simple request of each one.

At the appointed time, Lawrence returned to the præfectoria, making his way through the crowds who sat or stood on the steps. Approaching one of the guards at the top, he said politely, "Please tell the præfect that Lawrence has returned and has brought with him the treasure of the church. And tell him it is so great that he will have to come to the steps to receive it."

The guard inspected Lawrence, who carried nothing and was dressed in his usual threadbare homespun tunic. He looked puzzled and a little suspicious, but in the end he merely raised an eyebrow and departed into the hall.

The guard must have mentioned something of his suspicion to the præfect, for the fierce little man in the fine toga was already turning red when he came marching furiously out to the colonnaded portico. A smiling Lawrence beckoned him forward to the top of the steps and gave a grand sweep of his arm toward the crowd below.

The mob that slouched and sprawled on the broad marble stairway was not the usual merchants, noblemen, politicians, or city officials who had business there. Among them there was no gold or silver to be seen, no bolts of fine cloth, no chests full of plates, goblets, and bowls produced by gifted artisans.

Instead, the præfect saw steps jammed with the dregs of the slums—widows with their unruly, grimy-face broods; street urchins who curled up in the doorways of the shops to sleep at night and could be as dangerous as a pack of tiny wolves if met while one was alone; elderly day laborers whose skills were few; men missing limbs, having donated them to the glory of Rome on some distant battlefield; women whose bruises, weariness, and gaping clothes did more than hint at their occupation; and beggars blind, lame, and horribly disfigured. A few, even at this early hour, had clearly been at their wineskins steadily for some time past.

The præfect's red face was turning a dangerous shade of purple.

"Behold!" cried Lawrence with another dramatic gesture. "Here are the treasures of the church! Surely the church is rich, far richer than your emperor!"

The præfect, it turned out, didn't have much of a sense of humor. He immediately condemned Lawrence to a particularly nasty death—he had him roasted on a gridiron. Ambrose of Milan claimed that, during his torture, Lawrence cried out, "It is well done. Turn me over!"[2]

It's understandable, then, that Lawrence is regarded as the patron saint of comedians. And of librarians and archivists, because he went to great lengths to hide the books and documents of the church; and cooks and chefs, for obvious though grisly reasons. And especially of the poor, whom he so clearly loved and honored.

The story of the martyrdom of St. Lawrence, as I've told it, is full of details that can't be confirmed. The date of his death and those of Pope Sixtus II and the other six deacons are a matter of historical record, as is the Valerian persecution and the specific edict requiring the death of church leaders and the relinquishing of all church property to the Roman government. Sixtus and the six were executed on August 6; Lawrence was indeed put to death "after three days," on the tenth.

It seems very likely that he did ship the Communion cup, then just a small brown agate bowl, to his parents in Spain. It may still be seen in the Valencia Cathedral, although the simple bowl, which has been authenticated as dating to well before the time of Christ, is now set in an ornate framework that includes gold, pearls, and two handles so that it may be used without handling the bowl itself. There's a surprisingly cogent argument that it could, in fact, have been the cup Jesus passed to his disciples at the Last Supper.

The account of the exchange between Sixtus and Lawrence, as well as that between Lawrence and the præfect, date to accounts related generations later and so can't be reliably confirmed. The same is true of his being grilled and the joking instruction to his tormentors. Historians say beheading would have been more likely, but if he had really ticked the præfect off, who knows? The people who came up with crucifixion knew a thing or two about killing their enemies in humiliating and excruciating fashion.

Not many tales of early church martyrs are so darkly humorous. Whether these details are true or they were just added to make a great story even better, what is certain is what they convey about the church's vision of itself through the roughly four hundred years afterward while those stories were being told.[3]

The church's first responsibility was understood not to be an imperial or civil power or even to submit to them, but to stand with, and for, the poorest and most vulnerable people in society. It was not money or respectability or safety that mattered most, but the currency of relationship. At the very heart of the identity of the church were those people who were rejected and unvalued elsewhere.

This was how the church viewed itself for at least the first six or seven hundred years of its existence. As we saw in chapter 1, by the time Luther nailed his ninety-five theses to the door of All Saints' Church in Wittenberg on All Hallows' Eve, 1517, the church had become a tragic caricature of herself. She desperately needed a radical adjustment of her character.

The time is ripe for another such reformation.

What would it look like if we reformed ourselves to look like the Kingdom Jesus spoke about, if we lived the pure, undefiled religion James wrote about? How could we reshape our churches into real communities of faith in which Beatitudes people were viewed as the treasure of the church? Our church world would certainly be turned upside down. Anything could happen!

WE'D ACTUALLY FOLLOW JESUS

A little while ago, I was invited to meet with a small group of people from a church that wanted to learn how to reach out more effectively in its neighborhood. In an effort to "take the temperature" of the group and the church they represented, I asked, "What are the kinds of things we expect Jesus followers to do?" They grinned awkwardly, knowing as they spoke the words the answer was lame: "Pray and read your Bible every day, go to church, don't lie, be faithful to your spouse . . ."

"So what would we do if we actually did follow Jesus?"

After a short pause, this simple and profound response: "We'd go where he went and do what he did." Brilliant.

Where did he go?

From the place of ultimate power, privilege, and security, he went to an oppressed nation, a poor family among poor people, and the vulnerability of living among—speaking, walking, working, teaching, healing, challenging—people who would want what they could get from him, who would try to co-opt him for their own purposes, who would briefly adore and then criticize, betray, condemn, torture, and murder him. He sought out the people who did not deserve what he had to offer and the people whom nobody else wanted to get close to—the religiously "unclean," the diseased, the demon possessed, the traitors, the immoral, the foreigners, and even the oppressors.

He didn't stay safely in his village or save his religious passion for the synagogue. He went. Galilee, Samaria, the Decapolis, Judea—through the dusty hills, into bitter little redneck towns, among the tombs, into the city alleys and enclaves where the broken, the beggars, the discarded ones eked out their miserable existences. And before he left his disciples, he told them to go too. Out into the world.

If we were following Jesus, we'd be known as people who go to the dangerous, poor, unpleasant places. Not just a few select missionaries to other countries; we'd go as congregations, as communities of disciples—followers—to the most difficult spots in our own cities and towns.

What did he do?

He announced Good News for people who are poor and broken. He proclaimed God's pleasure in them. He taught the surprising, revolutionary character of the Kingdom of Heaven to people who were sure—until they heard him—that they didn't belong in it. He illustrated that Kingdom's character by feeding the hungry, healing the sick, touching the untouchable, casting out demons, and raising the dead. He overturned the money changers' tables; called out the leaders who promoted an empty, form-first religion; and refused to be intimidated by them or by the most powerful political and military empire in history. He laid down his life for the people he had come to call his friends.

Wouldn't we look different if we actually did what Jesus did? What would it look like if we, in our time and circumstances, "raised the dead" or "overturned the money changers' tables"? If we didn't just criticize the church, but instead went out there and actually lived as the body of Christ in the world? If we submitted our politics and economics to our religion, instead of the other way around, and gave our lives to raise up people who were hopeless, helpless, and lost, teaching them that the Kingdom belongs to them?

We'd be a dangerous people, a threat to the powers of this world. We'd be magnetic, intoxicating to be around. We'd be loving and joyful; we'd be the epicenter of a cultural and economic revolution. We'd be so comfortable eating and drinking with outcasts and sinners that we wouldn't be intimidated by the occasional invitation to do the same with the power brokers.

We'd be an irresistible force, lifting up those who have been oppressed, setting free those who have been imprisoned, returning sight to those who were blind—the power within us would liberate rather than dominate, create rather than consume, and render us vulnerable rather than unassailable.

Others would look at us and say, "So that's what Jesus looks like . . ."

WE'D PREACH A WHOLE, INTEGRATED GOSPEL

The Reformation became necessary because the gospel itself had become an amputee—the ability of the individual to approach God, and the necessity of a face-to-face personal salvation by faith alone, had been amputated and replaced with a prosthetic dogma: Only the church could administer salvation.

As we've already seen in our world today, the church in this regard tends to be divided primarily into two groups: those who stress a personal, private salvation and are wary of "social" justice; and those who see the gospel primarily as a message of social change and are wary of evangelical "enthusiasm" and commitment to personal holiness. The evil one has devised an enduring and effective strategy to diminish the power of the gospel preached by Jesus and the apostles: encourage Christians to grab just a piece of the gospel instead of the whole, and then argue about which piece is more important.

Our evangelical pastors need to begin preaching a *comprehensive theology of Kingdom justice* to their congregations. I don't mean a reference here or there or the occasional encouragement from the pulpit to engage in acts of random kindness. I mean a consistent, exhaustive, week-by-week exegesis that works through the Bible from start to finish, revealing God's concern, encouragement, and command that his people live justly and actively seek justice for others. Evangelicals need to understand that the Cross of Christ is the crux of Kingdom justice. It wouldn't hurt to take an entire year to do this, and there's more than enough material in Scripture! Of course, this means that some preachers will first have to learn that justice theology themselves. Making the investment in doing so will, I can assure them, be a richly rewarding experience as the beauty, power, and scope of the gospel of Jesus Christ expands in their understanding.

Our mainline ministers and priests, and others who have adopted what is regarded by some as a "liberal" approach to Christian faith and doctrine, need to begin preaching *the necessity and exciting vitality of a personal, passionate relationship with Jesus.* Comforting ritual, anonymous attendance, supporting worthy causes, and "good" living miss the point; as we've seen, those activities are in dramatic decline anyway. They will get some pushback; there are some congregations in which it is safer to mention the name of almost anyone than Jesus. A thorough examination of the Gospels would reveal him as the complex, deep, challenging, and endlessly attractive figure he is, whose invitation to follow him represents the most thrilling adventure life has to offer. People involved in a kindly but abstracted sort of "doing good" will discover a personal connection far deeper than they had imagined possible and a fuel to fire their societal engagement in a new and vital manner. I know people who began to follow Jesus as Teacher before they ever knew him as the Son of God. (This was certainly the case for all the original disciples!) God's justice in society begins with the encounter of the individual human soul with the Christ whose death and resurrection justifies us.

Disillusioned Christians who have discarded or drifted

away from conventional church need to seek out vital, communal expressions of their personal faith and commit themselves to living with the inevitable tensions and joys of sharing the journey with others. In other words, they need to recommit themselves to the body of Christ and to participation within it, even if they remain unable to attach themselves to conventional congregations. This would include a new or renewed determination to *investigate and share together what Scripture actually has to say about what the gospel is and how we are to live it together* in our local communities, our regions, our nations. This group may be the one that has the greatest potential to establish the character and principles of a new *ekklesia*—one which, like its Master, radically loves the world while not being bound or seduced by it.

If we're going to live it, we need to understand what we're living.

WE'D BE FOCUSED ON PRACTICAL JUSTICE

Of course, all justice is practical. If it isn't applied in real time in the real world, it ain't justice. The point here is that what we preach has to result in action. Sermons that encourage us in a general way to be courageous, explain why worship or prayer matters, review the life of "David: A Man After God's Own Heart," or follow the bland course supplied by sermon outline services[4] may be fine in a given context. But the lack of spiritual nutrition in them must certainly be contributing to the withering of the church, both numerically and in terms of its impact on the world around us.

The very reason for being, the core purpose of our congregations, would cease being about the comfort and encouragement of its own members and would shift instead to a focus on identifying, getting close to, and caring for people struggling with various manifestations of poverty in our own neighborhoods: destitution, oppression, depression, sickness, exclusion, vulnerability, and so on. The church was never supposed to be about itself; we would discover there is ample comfort and encouragement to be found in actually pursuing the church's biblical agenda.

We would discover that, rather than being our primary preoccupations, the church building and gatherings would function more like the base camp of a mountain-climbing expedition. Staying hunkered down in the base camp negates its very purpose. Neither is the church supposed to stay in the church. It is supposed to "go into all the world and preach the gospel to all creation."[5]

Go. Not "stay, and try to persuade people to come in." Go.

OUR ENERGIES WOULD BE DIRECTED OUTWARD

How much of the resources of most churches—the time and energy of congregants and church staff members, the money, the buildings and equipment—is devoted to providing services of one kind or another to people who are already part of the congregation? Eighty percent? Ninety? More?

Church leaders need to lead—that is, they need to go and do, trusting that others will follow, rather than staying, instructing, and sending. They need to make it clear that their own primary work is not to produce an excellent Sunday service but to be themselves out in the neighborhood, working among the poorest people there—that what they say and do on Sunday morning comes directly out of those activities. This needs not to be delegated to one outreach pastor, whose real work is to organize church members to do occasional volunteer work at other organizations. Identification of, outreach to, and pastoral care of the neediest people in the surrounding parish needs to be the core mission of the church and the core activity of the church's employees. This, surely, would require a radical culture shift in most churches.

In my experience, it's often the church's senior minister(s) who presents the greatest hurdle to a church taking a more Kingdom-oriented approach. Most of them got into ministry in the first place at least in part—and naturally enough—because they liked church culture as they experienced it and were attracted to the conventional kind of ministerial role they always saw modeled. Some are already so overwhelmed by the needs of their "normal" congregation that adding to the burden engagement with people whose needs are even greater just seems impossible. And so they limit their own role in "going into all the world" to equipping those who have to do so daily anyway.

But that has to change. Has to. A pastor whose role remains almost exclusively within the congregation and its weekly activities is sending a subtle but clear message that, after all, that's what is most spiritually important. Such a pastor needs to trust that God will answer his or her needs, and the needs of the congregation, if he or she answers the call of Jesus to go out. This is the path of faith.

A leader doesn't mobilize others and send them out. A leader goes out himself or herself. The others will follow.

WE'D BE COMMITTED TO COMMUNITY

Remember the church as described in the early chapters of Acts? Its members lived their lives together as a community and out in the larger community. Remember the crowd on the præfectoria steps? They were the treasure of the church, living together, not only Sunday by Sunday in the sanctuary but also day by day in the streets and slums of Rome.

The church would look not much like a social club that attracts mostly people of the same ilk, but instead like a diverse, motley group whose only real point of connection is the gospel of Jesus Christ. The Kingdom of God. We would breach social, economic, ethnic, and cultural barriers. We would find practical ways to be a seven-days-per-week community. We'd share food with one another and with others. Some would share their homes. We would support one another in trials and advocate for those experiencing injustice. The wealthy would discover just how blessedly poor they are, and the poor would find they are rich in unimaginable ways.

We'd find ourselves planting new churches in the poorest neighborhoods, instead of the ones that offer the best hope for financial self-sustainability. Some of us would decide that our big-box churches out in the suburbs are simply in the wrong place—we'd sell and move to a location that better reflects the true priorities of the gospel. Others would decide to repurpose the "campus" for a truly Kingdom agenda. We might, for instance, use all that space that sits mostly empty for five or six days a week to establish a Christian school—no, not another private school for privileged kids, but a school set up to give the very best education, training, mentoring, and encouragement toward higher education for kids from poor neighborhoods, whose own schools almost guarantee they will stay poor. One church I know turned half of its facility into the best shelter for homeless people in the region. There have to be dozens of such ways to turn our empty temples into real homes for the family of God.

We'd start figuring out how our job skills could be better used toward furthering the Kingdom of Heaven, even if it came at the cost of career advancement. We'd encourage our kids to choose careers because they can have an impact in the Kingdom, not because they offer the greatest opportunity for material gain. Our kids would thank us later, because they'd have benefited from something more fulfilling than money: meaning.

We would revisit and reimagine our family budgets, making our goal having enough instead of having more, so that we can share what God has given. We might move the family home, too, so that we can live among or in closer proximity to the Beatitudes people we have come to love. Our kids would grow up with the rich experience of knowing people who are struggling with the many challenges of poverty. They would understand that there is no *them* and there is only *us*; they would not take for granted their own privileges, succumbing to entitlement, nor would they feel guilty about them.

We would not keep silent when people who are poor are blamed for their poverty; when another young black man is unjustly shot and killed by police; when another First Nations woman goes missing and no investigation is begun; when supports for people who are addicted, mentally ill, or homeless are slashed again; when unjust laws that target people who are poor are passed. *We would claim those people as our brothers and sisters* and raise our voices in support. *We would abandon political-party allegiances and vote according to the gospel of our Lord Jesus Christ.* Those of us who are politicians or police officers or social workers or employees of banks and large corporations or military personnel or church workers would stand and speak loudly, if necessary as ones crying in the wilderness, about the injustice that infects the cultures within which we work and spreads to the world around us.

We would rethink the dynamics and ergonomics of the gatherings at which we worship, pray, and learn. We would not abandon gathering together—we'd long for it. Here, too, we would find ways to put at the center people whose poverty means that elsewhere they are unheard and unseen. We would listen to one another's prayers and worship, rich and poor, and we would learn a great deal from one another. We would discover the reality that we truly are brothers and sisters: kin. We would look one another in the eyes, instead of lining up to stare at the preacher or the worship team. There would be no audience, because all of us would be participants. And God would show up.

We would be *the church.*

Bone ligamented to bone, sheathed in strong muscle,

covered with flesh and glowing skin, blood coursing through the whole body propelled by a mighty heart, our lungs drawing in great breaths of the Spirit. We would act with the power and authority of the body of Christ in this world.

We would be alive, unashamedly living the true religion of James and Lawrence—the religion of Jesus Christ.

And now, as our Lord has taught us, let us pray that it may be so:

> **Our Father**
>> *Father of us all, who gathers us together as children of one family, longing for connection and for home*
>
> **Who is in heaven**
>> *Who rules the heavens, our home, and is the source of all heavenly values and might*
>
> **Hallowed be your name**
>> *You are all that is holy and good; may everyone come to know it*
>
> **Your kingdom come**
>> *Our sick world needs your justice now, right now*
>
> **Your will be done**
>> *We know you desire it, and we want to live it*
>
> **On earth as it is in heaven**
>> *Here and now, empower us to live the reality of the Kingdom of Heaven on earth*
>
> **Give us today our daily bread**
>> *We depend on you for what we need to live today and every day . . .*

Forgive us our debts
We know we owe you everything

As we forgive those who are indebted to us
*Help us to give and forgive as graciously and
generously as you do*

Lead us not into temptation
*You know how easily we succumb to our selfish
desires*

But deliver us from evil
*And you know how vulnerable we are to the
oppressive systems of this world*

For the kingdom is yours
*You've told us who belongs within it, and we can
hardly believe it's us*

The power and the glory
*Liberation instead of domination, shining through
the dirt*

Now and forever
For us in our time, and through all eternity . . .

Say "amen," somebody.

appendix

the beatitudes, paraphrased

THIS IS MY PARAPHRASE OF THE BEATITUDES—what I think those crowds of sick, desperate people thronging around Jesus on the hillside might have understood him to say:

> Blessed are the spiritually bankrupt, for all the riches of the Kingdom are available to bail them out.
> Blessed are those whose life is a litany of loss and destruction and who are so blasted by grief they cannot stand, for they will find a new and strengthening intimacy among others who grieve and with the Comforter by their side.
> Blessed are the shoved out, put down, and ripped off, for they will discover that everything—everything!—belongs to them and nothing can restrain them.
> Blessed are those who are starving for justice, dying of thirst for someone to treat them right, for a feast is coming.

Blessed are the guilty ones who, knowing their own
guilt, show mercy to others; they'll receive mercy
too.

Blessed are those whose whole being—body, soul,
and spirit—is so focused on discovering God for
themselves that nothing in this world ever seems
good enough; they'll find what they've been
looking for at last.

Blessed are the ones who stand in the middle of other
people's disputes and are hated by both sides;
it's a horrible place to be, but it's where they are
claiming their identity as children of God.

Blessed are those who are battered and bruised because
they try to treat others well; they are displaying
their citizenship in the Kingdom of God here and
now.[1]

acknowledgments

VIRTUALLY EVERYTHING I've ever published is the fruit of my own formation within and by the Sanctuary community in Toronto, and of sharing in the formation of that community as a whole. I won't even try to list the names, because there would be hundreds. Suffice to say that this book, as do my others, owes its essence to Sanctuary's "anchor" and "core" community members, staff, board, and supporters. They have not only taught me what I've been learning but have also given me the freedom and support necessary to write.

Dan, Les, and Doug have been walking this path with me for more than thirty years. Miller and Terri Alloway, along with the Maranatha Foundation, have been my patrons—and promoters!—for more than a decade. I would be a long way from even beginning to work on this present book if not for their generosity and friendship.

Tim Huff, another recipient of their graciousness, has been my writing buddy throughout that period—a companionship that helps keep me focused and relieves the strange combination of tedium and pressure that builds up when you spend a couple of weeks at a time writing for eight to ten hours a day.

I owe a debt of thanks to Greg Daniel, my agent, and Don Pape, my publisher, who continue to show faith in my work despite less than inspiring sales. The insightful editing of David Zimmerman and Helen Macdonald has, no question, made this a better book than it would have been.

The writing and ministry lives of Henri Nouwen, Jean Vanier, John Perkins, Ray Bakke, Robert Lupton, Dallas Willard, and Kenneth Bailey continue to shape both my thinking and praxis, and have had particular influence on this book. Many thanks, too, to Leonard Sweet for his support, writing, and endorsements.

Sometimes a parent wonders who is shaping whom. My wife and I have seven kids, two daughters-in-law, and a grandchild between us, so there's been a lot of shaping going on. I'm grateful for each of them and for our sometimes convoluted life together.

Finally, there's Maggie—best friend, bride and lover, partner and companion on the journey. I couldn't ask for more, better, or sweeter.

My deepest gratitude to all of you.

notes

INTRODUCTION
1. See Matthew 5:17.
2. John 14:15, ESV.

CHAPTER ONE: *bad religion*
1. James 1:26.
2. Alan Hirsch, *The Forgotten Ways: Reactivating the Missional Church* (Grand Rapids, MI: Brazos, 2006), 18–19.
3. Consider Thomas Asbridge, *The Crusades: The Authoritative History of the War for the Holy Land* (New York: HarperCollins, 2010). The subtitle presents a bold claim for a one-volume account, but it's highly readable and covers the main era and theater of the Crusades, and the opening line makes it clear that the battles had nothing to do with the Crusaders protecting hearth and home, as some have recently tried to claim.
4. Martin Luther, *On the Jews and Their Lies*, quoted in Robert Michael, "Luther, Luther Scholars, and the Jews," *Encounter* 46, no. 4 (Autumn 1985): 343–44.
5. Frank Newport, "Protestants and Frequent Churchgoers Most Supportive of Iraq War," Gallup, March 16, 2006, http://www.gallup.com/poll/21937/protestants-frequent-churchgoers-most-supportive-iraq-war.aspx. And Aaron James, "Report Claims Blair's Christian Faith Influenced Iraq War Decision," *Premier*, July 6, 2016, https://www.premier.org.uk/News/UK/Report-claims-Blair-s-Christian-faith-influenced-Iraq-War-decision. This report indicates that Prime Minister Tony Blair supported the US initiative in part, at least, because of his "Christian" convictions.
6. Max Fisher, "Map: How 35 Countries Compare on Child Poverty (the U.S. Is Ranked 34th)," *Washington Post*, April 15, 2013, http://www.washingtonpost.com/blogs/worldviews/wp/2013/04/15/map-how-35-countries-compare-on-child-poverty-the-u-s-is-ranked-34th/. This United Nations Children's Fund report shows the child poverty rate in the United States is 23 percent. For Canada and the United Kingdom, it's under 15 percent.
7. Sophia Kerby, "The Top 10 Most Startling Facts about People of Color and Criminal Justice in the United States: A Look at the Racial Disparities Inherent in Our Nation's Criminal-Justice System," Center for American Progress, March 13, 2012, accessed May 16, 2017, http://www.americanprogress.org/issues/race/news/2012/03/13/11351/the-top-10-most-startling-facts-about-people-of-color-and-criminal-justice-in-the-united-states/. One in three African American men can expect to be

incarcerated during their lifetimes. African Americans represent about 30 percent of the general population and 60 percent of the incarcerated population.

8. Mia Dauvergne, "Adult Correctional Statistics in Canada, 2010/2011," Statistics Canada, updated October 12, 2012, accessed May 16, 2017, http://www.statcan.gc.ca/pub/85-002-x/2012001/article/11715-eng.htm#a7. The report states that "27% of adults in provincial and territorial custody and 20% of those in federal custody involved Aboriginal people, about *seven to eight times higher* than the proportion of Aboriginal people (3%) in the adult population as a whole" (emphasis added).

9. See Richard Twiss, *Rescuing the Gospel from the Cowboys: A Native American Expression of the Jesus Way* (Downers Grove, IL: InterVarsity, 2015) for a pithy summary and indictment of the church's participation in this shameful business.

10. See 1 John 3:16.

11. Although I have obscured his identity elsewhere, I have written about Mike in some of my other books.

12. Mike passed away, at peace, in his own apartment, on July 30, 2016. He was, as he said often to me in those last months, "ready to go home." About 150 people attended his memorial, including the Jones House boys.

CHAPTER TWO: *spiritual or religious?*

1. "Growth of the Nonreligious," Pew Research Center, July 2, 2013, accessed May 17, 2017, http://www.pewforum.org/2013/07/02/growth-of-the-nonreligious-many-say-trend-is-bad-for-american-society/.

2. "2011 National Household Survey: Immigration, Place of Birth, Citizenship, Ethnic Origin, Visible Minorities, Language and Religion," Statistics Canada, updated May 9, 2013, accessed July 18, 2017, http://www.statcan.gc.ca/daily-quotidien/130508/dq130508b-eng.htm?HPA.

3. Emma White, "Religion in England and Wales 2011," Office for National Statistics, December 11, 2012, accessed July 18, 2017, https://www.ons.gov.uk peoplepopulationandcommunity/culturalidentity/religion/articles/religioninenglandandwales2011/2012-12-11#changing-picture-of-religious-affiliation-over-last-decade.

4. Robert Ricciardelli, "God Transforming Lives, a 10-Stop Journey by George Barna," *Patheos: The Converging Zone*, March 17, 2017, accessed May 17, 2017, http://www.patheos.com/blogs/robertricciardelli/faith/god-transforming-lives-a-10-stop-journey-by-george-barna/.

5. "Three Spiritual Journeys of Millennials," Barna, June 3, 2013, https://www.barna.com/research/three-spiritual-journeys-of-millennials/.

6. Not their real names.

7. See Ephesians 6:15.

8. See Philippians 2:12-13.
9. Acts 4:32.
10. Romans 8:20-22, ESV.
11. Colossians 1:20, ESV.
12. Luke 4:18.
13. Ibid.
14. See 1 John 4:8, 16.
15. From the Latin uni ("one") and com ("with"). See also *Merriam-Webster's* definition at https://www.merriam-webster.com/dictionary/community.
16. From the Latin *forma* ("shape") and *con* ("together, with"), inferring "with the [same] shape" or "shaped together." See also *Merriam-Webster's* definition at https://www.merriam-webster.com/dictionary/conformity.
17. John 13:34; 15:12, 17, ESV.
18. Paul Muggeridge, "Which Countries Produce the Most Waste," World Economic Forum, August 20, 2015, https://www.weforum.org/agenda/2015/08/which-countries-produce-the-most-waste/.
19. Galatians 5:22-23, 25.
20. Matthew 6:10, KJV.
21. See Matthew 25:34-40.

CHAPTER THREE: *dry bones*

1. See 1 Corinthians 15:7.
2. See especially Acts 15:13-21 and Galatians 2:9-10.
3. See Matthew 5:17.
4. Mark 2:27.
5. Mark 12:18-20.
6. James 1:26-27.
7. See Matthew 6:16-18.
8. Isaiah 58:3-7, emphasis added.
9. For example: Leviticus 10:13, 14; Deuteronomy 18:3.
10. Matthew 6:33, ESV.
11. Acts 26:5.
12. Colossians 2:18-19.
13. James 1:26-27.
14. *Online Etymology Dictionary*, s.v. "religion," http://www.etymonline.com/index.php?term=religion.
15. *Online Etymology Dictionary*, s.v. "ligament," http://www.etymonline.com/index.php?allowed_in_frame=0&search=ligament.
16. Ezekiel 37:1-3.
17. Ezekiel 37:4-6.
18. Ezekiel 37:9-10.

CHAPTER FOUR: *bad religion can feel so good*

1. See Jeremiah 32:35.
2. John 7:5.
3. Luke 8:19, 21.
4. Mark 6:2-3, emphasis added.
5. See Mark 6:5.
6. See 1 Corinthians 15:4-7.
7. There are likely at least three different people called James in the New Testament, and they're not always clearly distinguished from one another. It's hard to know for sure who did what and when.
8. See Galatians 1:19.
9. Alexander Roberts and James Donaldson, eds., *The Ante-Nicene Fathers: Translations of the Writings of the Fathers Down to A.D. 325*, vol. 8, (New York: C. Scribner's Sons, 1903), 218.
10. Hegesippus, "Fragments from His Five Books of Commentaries on the Acts of the Church," Early Christian Writings, http://www .earlychristianwritings.com/text/hegesippus.html.
11. The "Charlie Hebdo" attack in 2015. Other attacks have killed many more since, polarizing Muslims as well as Christians.
12. Jack Sommers, "Murdered Police Officer Ahmed Merabet's Brother Malek Says Charlie Hebdo Terrorists 'Pretend to Be Muslims,'" *Huffington Post*, January 12, 2015, http://www.huffingtonpost.com/2015/01/12/ahmed -merabet_n_6456328.html.
13. James 1:1. This is one of the reasons some commentators think somebody else wrote it. But on a number of levels, I think it makes perfect sense that he doesn't trade on his status. To do so, in fact, would be counter to what he teaches in the letter itself. His introduction is beautifully humble—an example of living out what Jesus taught.

CHAPTER FIVE: *believe it or not*

1. Luke 8:21.
2. James 1:22-25.
3. Matthew 15:8-9.
4. James 2:12-13.
5. Luke 10:27-28, paraphrased.
6. John 13:34; 15:12.
7. John 8:36.
8. Luke 9:23-24.
9. Luke 9:25-26.
10. James 2:14-17.
11. Matthew 25:40.

12. Vanessa R. Wight, Michelle Chau, and Yumiko Aratani, "Who Are America's Poor Children?: The Official Story," January 2010, National Center for Children in Poverty, http://www.nccp.org/publications/pdf /text_912.pdf, 3.
13. Campaign 2000, "Let's Do This; Let's End Child Poverty for Good: 2015 Report Card on Child and Family Poverty in Canada," Family Service Toronto, http://campaign2000.ca/wp-content/uploads/2016/03/C2000 -National-Report-Card-Nov2015.pdf.
14. James 2:18-19.
15. James 4:17.
16. See Matthew 21:28-31.
17. A critical part of the founding and early life of Sanctuary as a community was the work of a band called Red Rain, of which I am a member. Some of that story can be found in my earlier books.
18. James 2:16.

CHAPTER SIX: *living the beatitudes*

1. James 1:27.
2. James 2:5.
3. Matthew 5:3-10, emphasis added.
4. Kenneth E. Bailey, *Jesus through Middle Eastern Eyes: Cultural Studies in the Gospels* (Downers Grove, IL: InterVarsity, 2008), 68.
5. Matthew 20:16.
6. In particular, "dispensationalism."
7. See Matthew 4:23-25.
8. *Strong's Concordance*, s.v. *"ptócho,"* http://biblehub.com/greek/4434 .htm.
9. Matthew 11:29.
10. Exodus 22:22-24, ESV, emphasis added.
11. See John 18:28.
12. James 2:1-9.
13. Galatians 2:10. Paul comments that this was "the very thing I was eager to do."
14. James 2:6-7.
15. See Mark 10:17-31.
16. Matthew 23:13. Almost the entire chapter is a blistering rant against the false religion practiced by the Pharisees.
17. Matthew 23:25.
18. Matthew 23:16-17.
19. Luke 18:24.
20. I told this story on my blog. Greg Paul, "Eulogy for the Ones Who Never

Had a Chance," *Sanctuary* (blog), March 4, 2016, http://sanctuarytoronto
.ca/2016/03/04/eulogy-for-the-ones-who-never-had-a-chance/.

21. Matthew 4:24.

CHAPTER SEVEN: *the leveling effect*

1. Luke 3:4-6, quoting from Isaiah 40:3-5.

2. Jennifer Wells, "Lost Boy: The Death of Darcy Allan Sheppard," *Toronto Star*, December 26, 2013, https://www.thestar.com/news/insight/2013/12/26/lost_boy_the_death_of_darcy_allan_sheppard.html.

3. James 5:1-6.

4. Furthermore, the mere fact that you, whoever you are, are reading this suggests that you also may be a rich person. Even if you don't feel as if you are. If you slept in your own bed last night, aren't afraid of losing your place at the end of the month, and don't ever really worry about where your next meal is coming from, you're wealthier than most people in this world. According to www.globalrichlist.com, if your entire income from all sources last year exceeded $20,000 (US), you're in the top 3.65 percent in the world. About 220 million people make more than that, but that leaves more than 7 billion who do not.

5. Two other interpretations of this saying are commonly offered: (1) There was a gate known colloquially as "the Eye of the Needle." Because it was so narrow, it required camels to be stripped of their burdens before being able to pass through. This gate is supposed to have been found in Jerusalem itself, or in Damascus, but has proved impossible to confirm and may be apocryphal. (2) The Aramaic word Jesus would have used is the same for both *camel* and *rope*. Greek translators may not have been aware of this and assumed he meant *camel*, when in fact he meant *rope*. Clearly, you can't thread a needle with a rope—although you probably could with a strand of the fiber from which the rope was made. Both interpretations strengthen the necessity of being divested of dependence on wealth in order to enter into the Kingdom of God. The second interpretation is a slightly gentler form of the humor I posit here.

6. See Luke 9:46; 22:24.

7. See 2 Corinthians 8:9.

8. James 1:10-11.

9. Luke 14:12-14.

10. Matthew 19:26.

11. James 1:9.

12. Acts 4:32.

13. Acts 4:33-34.

14. Luke 18:10-14.

15. James 4:4.

16. James 4:10.
17. Barna Group, "Americans Are Misinformed about Poverty, but Widely Involved in Helping the Poor," Barna, June 25, 2007, https://www.barna .com/research/americans-are-misinformed-about-poverty-but-widely -involved-in-helping-the-poor/.
18. James 2:8-9.
19. Galatians 3:26-28.
20. Frank and Louise are not the individuals' real names.

CHAPTER EIGHT: *watch your mouth!*
1. James 1:26.
2. James 1:19-21.
3. "James 1:21," *Interlinear Bible*, http://biblehub.com/interlinear/james/1-21. htm.
4. James 3:3-5.
5. James 3:5-6.
6. Mark 7:6-7, 9, emphasis added.
7. See James 3:7-8.
8. Mark 7:20-23.
9. See Luke 12:16-21.
10. James 4:1-3.
11. James 5:12, emphasis added.
12. Luke 6:27-28.
13. Acts 15:1.
14. Acts 15:5.
15. Acts 15:8-11.
16. See Acts 11:1-17.
17. Acts 10:11.
18. Acts 10:13.
19. Acts 10:14.
20. Acts 10:15.
21. Acts 10: 26, 28.
22. Acts 10:34-35.
23. Acts 15:13-15, 19.
24. Acts 15:31.
25. See Matthew 13:24-29.

CHAPTER NINE: *the surprise in submission*
1. Karl Marx, "Critique of Hegel's Philosophy of Right." Originally published as an essay in *Deutsch-Französische Jahrbücher* (Paris, February 1844). The popular quotation "Religion is the opiate of the masses" isn't accurate. Here's the context: "Religious suffering is, at one and the same

time, the expression of real suffering and a protest against real suffering. Religion is the sigh of the oppressed creature, the heart of a heartless world, and the soul of soulless conditions. It is the opium of the people." See, for example, https://www.marxists.org/archive/marx/works /download/Marx_Critique_of_Hegels_Philosophy_of_Right.pdf.

2. James 1:1.
3. James 1:2-4.
4. John 15:1-2, 5, 9-11.
5. Mark 15:34.
6. James 1:5-6.
7. James 1:12.
8. See James 1:13-16.
9. Mark 7:23.
10. James 4:1-4.
11. See Galatians 2:11-21.
12. James 4:7-10.
13. James 4:13-15.
14. The ancient Hebrew title of God, *El Shaddai*, is usually translated as "Almighty," but it's a poor translation that reveals our predilection for dominative power. A better rendering would be, as here, "All-Sufficient," because the word indicates the powerful, complete sufficiency of a nursing mother for her infant.
15. James 5:7-8.
16. I used to be much clearer on this. But my earlier eschatological beliefs are among many convictions I've had to release in submission to a God who grows daily bigger and more difficult to explain by theological/doctrinal systems.
17. See Matthew 13:24-30.
18. Matthew 25:34-36, 40.

CHAPTER TEN: *a twenty-first-century reformation*

1. Lawrence's hometown, in what is now northern Spain.
2. Leonard Foley, OFM, ed., "Lawrence," *Saint of the Day, Lives, Lessons, and Feasts,* revised by Pat McCloskey, OFM (Cincinnati, OH: St. Anthony Messenger Press, 2009), 228–29.
3. The first "complete" account of the martyrdom of St. Lawrence, as related here, dates to the seventh century. Fragments of the story can be found in various sources throughout the intervening 350–400 years.
4. If you weren't aware of this, search "sermon outlines" on the Web. You'll be astonished.
5. Mark 6:15.

APPENDIX: *the beatitudes, paraphrased*

1. God bless Dallas Willard, gone too soon, whose work in *The Divine Conspiracy*, together with that of Kenneth Bailey's in *Jesus through Middle Eastern Eyes*, inspired and (alongside simple lexical study of the text) informed this admittedly very "free" version of the Beatitudes.

about the author

GREG PAUL lives in Toronto, Canada, and is a pastor and founding member of Sanctuary, a faith community in which both the wealthy and the poor live, work, and share their experiences and resources daily. The Sanctuary community makes a priority of welcoming and caring for some of the most hurting and excluded people in Canada's largest city, including people struggling with addiction, mental illness, prostitution, and homelessness.

Greg is the author of four previous books: *Close Enough to Hear God Breathe, The Twenty-Piece Shuffle, God in the Alley,* and *Simply Open.*

THE NAVIGATORS® STORY

---○---

THANK YOU for picking up this NavPress book! I hope it has been a blessing to you.

NavPress is a ministry of The Navigators. The Navigators began in the 1930s, when a young California lumberyard worker named Dawson Trotman was impacted by basic discipleship principles and felt called to teach those principles to others. He saw this mission as an echo of 2 Timothy 2:2: "And the things you have heard me say in the presence of many witnesses entrust to reliable people who will also be qualified to teach others" (NIV).

In 1933, Trotman and his friends began discipling members of the US Navy. By the end of World War II, thousands of men on ships and bases around the world were learning the principles of spiritual multiplication by the person-to-person teaching of God's Word.

After World War II, The Navigators expanded its ministry to include college campuses; local churches; the Glen Eyrie Conference Center and Eagle Lake Camps in Colorado Springs, Colorado; and neighborhood and citywide initiatives across the country and around the world.

Today, with more than 2,600 US staff members—and local ministries in more than 100 countries—The Navigators continue the process of making disciples who make more disciples, advancing the Kingdom of God in a world that desperately needs the hope and salvation of Jesus Christ and the encouragement to grow deeper in relationship with Him.

NavPress was created in 1975 to advance the calling of The Navigators by bringing biblically rooted and culturally relevant products to people who want to know and love Christ more deeply. In January 2014, NavPress entered into an alliance with Tyndale House Publishers to strengthen and better position our rich content for the future. Through *The Message* Bible and other resources, NavPress seeks to bring positive spiritual movement to people's lives.

If you're interested in learning more or becoming involved with The Navigators, go to www.navigators.org. For more discipleship content from The Navigators and NavPress authors, visit www.thedisciplemaker.org. May God bless you in your walk with Him!

Sincerely,

DON PAPE
VP/PUBLISHER, NAVPRESS

www.navpress.com

CP1308